Functions
in Free Format
RPG IV

Functions
in Free Format
RPG IV

Jim Martin

MC PRESS

MC Press Online, LP
Lewisville, TX 75077

Functions in Free Format RPG IV
Jim Martin

First Edition

First Printing—May 2009

© 2009 Jim Martin. All rights reserved.

MC Press offers excellent discounts on this book when ordered in quantity for bulk purchases or special sales, which may include custom covers and content particular to your business, training goals, marketing focus, and branding interest.

For information regarding permissions or special orders, please contact:
MC Press
Corporate Offices
125 N. Woodland Trail
Lewisville, TX 75077 USA

For information regarding sales and/or customer service, please contact:
MC Press
P.O. Box 4300
Big Sandy, TX 75755-4300 USA

ISBN: 978-158347-087-9

To Jody,
my lovely wife,
who has inspired and motivated me
to continue on, sacrificing much in the process.

Acknowledgements

A hearty thank you to Hans Bolt and George Farr, IBM, who were very much involved in the creation of free-format RPG IV.

I would like to thank the management and staff of *Jack Henry & Associates* who supported me in the testing of my RPG IV code examples. Thanks especially to Mike Greenhaw and Tim Boettler.

My co-workers have been a tremendous help in my advancement in the knowledge and practical use of RPG IV and ILE. Thanks to Dave Farris, John Thomas, Johnny Carcioppolo, Millie Gray, Scott Jack, Gregory Simmons, Jeremy Willman, and Mike Tharp. There are countless more that have made a difference, and although I have regretfully omitted your name here, I am still in your debt.

I would be remiss if I didn't thank a few well known RPG and ILE instructors, who have helped me for many years. I consider it an honor to call you my friends: Jon Paris, Susan Gantner, and Kevin Forsythe.

And to Merrikay, Marianne, and the entire staff at MC Press, who add their literary and publishing skills, and shape my words and ideas into a book: thank you.

Contents

Preface

In my previous book, *Free Format RPG IV*, I explained differences in coding RPG IV: from legacy fixed-format, to the relatively new free-format. From the many conversations I have enjoyed with those of you attending the COMMON conferences, I believe that today free-format RPG IV has become the favored choice of most RPG IV programmers.

In my previous book, I touched on some of the built-in functions. In this book, I will expand on that subject, as well as look at other related topics, such as sub-procedures, ILE (Integrated Language Environment) topics, C functions, and modular "functional" programming. RPG IV programming standards are an important part of any programming "shop." Appendix A provides a suggested list of standards for you to consider.

I am convinced that by using these methods and techniques you will become more productive in writing and maintaining RPG IV programs.

—*Jim Martin*
May 2009

1

An Introduction to Functions

Make it right before you make it faster.
—Brian Kernighan and P. J. Plauger

The word "function" has been used for decades in the world of computer science. However, it was not used in the niche world of RPG programming until the mid-1990s. This is when the term "built-in function" entered the RPG programmer's lexicon, with the advent of RPG IV. The term was not altogether new, since Control Language (CL) had used the built-in functions %SST (substring) and %BIN (convert binary), and nearly all RPG programmers also write CL programs.

Today, the word "function" is used regularly in RPG technical manuals, articles, and presentations. Since a word can have many possible meanings, this chapter starts by defining "function" in the context of the RPG IV application development environment, and then compares a function to an operation code. The last section of this chapter breaks down a function into its two main components: a return value and parameters.

What Is a Function?

According to Merriam-Webster's dictionary, a function is defined as follows:

> *A computer subroutine; specifically: one that performs a calculation with variables provided by a program and supplies the program with a single result*

This definition begs for a definition of "subroutine." Here it is, this time from Dictionary.com:

A sequence of instructions for performing a particular task. Most programming languages, including most machine languages, allow the programmer to define subroutines. This allows the subroutine code to be called from multiple places, even from within itself (in which case it is called recursive). The programming language implementation takes care of returning control to (just after) the calling location, usually with the support of call and return instructions at machine language level. Most languages also allow arguments to be passed to the subroutine, and one, or occasionally more, return values to be passed back.

A function is often very similar to a subroutine, the main difference being that it is called chiefly for its return value, rather than for any side effects.

In the RPG IV language, subroutines use global variables, so they do not need parameters. Also, subroutines in RPG do not return anything, since programs can access all global variables. With the advent of RPG IV, the subprocedure facility meets most of the dictionary definition of a subroutine or function. You can pass parameters to a subprocedure and get one return value. Also, a subprocedure can call itself recursively, if desired.

RPG IV has two types of subroutines: the legacy version already discussed (dating from the early 1970s), and the new form, called a subprocedure. Together, these two types of subroutines provide programmers with the tools needed to modularize programs.

A function is similar to a procedure in that it has parameters and performs a particular task. The main difference between a function and a procedure is that a function has a return value. A review of RPG IV's built-in functions (BIFs) shows that most, but not all, meet the definition of a function exactly. If you have explored the capabilities of RPG IV subprocedures, you could accurately describe those with return values as "functions."

Functions vs. Operation Codes

It's not easy to compare functions and operation codes (*op-codes*), so let me break it down. Could functions be considered op-codes? The answer is somewhere between "no" and "sort of." Generally, an op-code performs something that is multi-step and fairly complex. For example, an I/O operation such as Read must do the following:

- Use one or more parameters (such as key arguments or a file name) to interface with the operating system.

- Wait for a response.

- Move data to fields and possibly to data structures.

In the case where end-of-file is reached, the op-code does not move data; instead, it sets an internal end-of-file flag. There is also the possibility of a record lock if the specified file has a file type of update. The Read op-code, then, is very complex.

How about the For op-code? It has many possible parameters. Upon entry, it must set its index, check to see if the index exceeds the limit imposed by a parameter, and determine where to go next—whether to go to the next sequential instruction or the instruction after Endfor. The For op-code, then, is also complex.

Prior to free-format RPG IV, there were many simple op-codes, such as sqrt, scan, cat, and subst. These simple, single-purpose op-codes become BIFs in free-format. Simple math operations became expression symbols, such as + (the plus sign) for addition and - (the minus sign) for subtraction.

Since built-in functions now perform the work previously done by op-codes, does that somehow make BIFs op-codes? No, but it reveals something about the modern RPG language. RPG has evolved from a fill-in-the-blanks report writer, to an operation-rich language, to the highly "functional" language that it is today.

Return Values

The preceding pages used the term "return value" without fully explaining the concept. It's time to do that now.

You probably know what a parameter is, and have passed parameters to a called program. Upon return, the value of one or more of the parameters might have changed. You might wonder, is this a return value? A parameter that changes its value when returning to the called program? The answer is no, not at all.

A simple BIF will help illustrate the concept of a return value. Here is a Read followed by a check for end-of-file:

```
Read filename;

If %eof(filename);
```

In this example, a Read operation is performed. Either a record is retrieved and placed in storage, or end-of-file is found. The If operation checks the value of its expression for true (or one). The expression is the BIF %eof, with the file name as a parameter. This BIF has a return value of data type indicator, which means that if we are not at end-of-file, the return value is zero. If we are at end-of-file, the return value is one. The return value *replaces* the BIF. In effect, then, the code would be either this:

```
If  '0';
```

or this:

```
If  '1';
```

In the first case, *If '0'* translates to false, so the If clause is bypassed. In the second case, *If '1'* translates to true, so the If clause is entered and performed.

Return values can be any data type, including indicator, character string, pointer, decimal, integer, date, and others. For example, the %alloc BIF returns a pointer data type. The %trim BIF returns a character string, and the %lookup BIF returns an unsigned integer. (BIF return values are explained in more detail in Chapter 2.)

When you write your own subprocedure, you can choose to have a return value of any data type. If you specify a return value, the subprocedure will have all the characteristics of a function, and the return value will be just as valid as with built-in functions. (Writing subprocedures is described in detail in Chapter 4.)

Function Parameters

As mentioned earlier, functions typically have parameters, also called *arguments*. The purpose of these parameters is to give the function a broader range of capability. For example, let's say you write a function (subprocedure) that returns the sales tax for your city and state. This function uses one parameter, a decimal amount field holding the total price (as input). As your business grows, you might need to compute the sales tax for other city/state combinations. By adding a city/state parameter to your function, you keep the sales-tax computation in one place. The function is given more breadth by having the additional parameter. Another way to explain this is to say the function has greater *utility*.

As another example, consider the %lookup BIF:

```
%Lookup(argument:array_name{:starting_index{:number
of elements}})
```

This BIF is the array lookup function for an equal match between the first parameter and the array specified in the second parameter. A third parameter is for specifying a starting index (other than one). There is also a fourth parameter in the %lookup BIF that never existed in the Lookup op-code. This parameter specifies how many elements to search before stopping. If this parameter is not specified, the default value is the total number of elements defined for the array. The return value is an unsigned integer of the index of the element that matches the argument. Zero is returned if no match is found.

Most of the time, the default value for the fourth parameter is fine, but if you are using an array based on dynamic storage, you really need that fourth parameter. Therefore, the %lookup BIF has more capability than the op-code it replaced.

Validity checking of function parameters is done by the system for BIFs and by the prototype process for subprocedures and other called procedures. It's always possible to supply a valid parameter to a function, but provide a value that is invalid. It is up to the function to reject values that cannot be used in the function, requiring run-time error messages.

At some point in your development of functions, you might find yourself designing a function with eight, 10, or more parameters. At this point, I suggest you stop and ask yourself, why so many parameters? Perhaps your function, while returning just one value, is too large in its scope. For example, suppose you want to write a function that returns net pay, in a payroll application. That doesn't seem too difficult, until you realize how many parameters you'll need, including gross pay, marital status, exemptions claimed (both state and federal), federal taxes, state taxes, non-taxed deductions such as 401K and 503B, and many more. The determination of net pay, then, is not as easy as it first seemed. Perhaps you could still write the calculation as a module or subroutine. You could also write functions for federal income tax and state income tax.

Be careful not to write functions that require too many parameters. My rule of thumb is to keep the number of parameters under 10. An alternative is to write the big routines as modules, use ILE binding, and implement export/import for variables instead of a large number of parameters.

Summary

Functions are the next frontier in coding RPG IV. Break down your work and use RPG's BIFs as much as possible. Write your own functions in the form of subprocedures. Write code in smaller units, and use ILE to bind the pieces and provide excellent performance. Use the "return value" concept liberally, including nesting of functions within functions.

The next chapter provides examples of nesting BIFs. This concept works just as well for your own functions (subprocedures).

Essential BIFs in Free-Format RPG IV

Don't sacrifice clarity for small gains in efficiency.
—Brian Kernighan and P. J. Plauger

In the 2001 definition of free-format RPG IV, many fixed-format operations were removed. There is still controversy over the removal of many popular operation codes, notably Move, Movel, and MoveA. My first book, *Free-Format RPG IV* (MC Press, 2005), addressed this situation. Overall, however, most RPG programmers (even the old-timers) have come to appreciate the virtues of free-format.

As of V6.1 of the i operating system, there are 116 fixed-format op-codes, but only 61 free-format op-codes. Many of the "missing" op-codes have been replaced with one or more built-in functions (BIFs). For example, the SUBST op-code is now the %subst BIF, in free-format. The LOOKUP op-code could be any of 10 BIFs in free-format RPG IV! In other words, if you write programs in free-format RPG IV, you *must* use BIFs to accomplish the needs of your programs. It's clear that a paradigm shift in RPG IV programming has occurred, away from an op-code style coding environment. Embracing the free-format style of programming means embracing function-oriented coding.

Different Uses for Built-in Functions

Built-in functions provide an essential part of free-format procedures. BIFs provide some new programming capabilities, as well as just doing the work previously performed by op-codes or resulting indicators. An important use of BIFs is the role they play in definition specifications. Many BIFs are referenced in the remainder of this chapter. For more details on these BIFs, refer to Appendix B in this book.

BIFs Used in Definition Specifications

At compile time, six BIFs can be used to help set initial values or the dimension size for arrays.

The %size BIF

The %size BIF returns the number of bytes of the named parameter. If the second parameter, *All, is specified, the total number of bytes of an array or data structure is returned. This BIF can be used as the value of the INZ keyword or the DIM keyword.

Here is an example:

```
D Name          S                  30
D Namelen       S                  5u 0           Inz(%size(Name))
D Array         S                  1              Dim(%size(Name))
```

In this example, the variable Namelen is initialized to 30, the size of the parameter Name. The variable Array (an array) is defined with 30 elements.

Be extra careful with %size. It returns the number of bytes, which is different than the length for many data types. The examples in Appendix B illustrate the values returned for different data types.

The %len BIF

The %len BIF returns an unsigned integer of the defined or current length of a field. This BIF can be used in setting an initial value (with the INZ keyword) or a dimension size (with the DIM keyword).

Here is an example:

```
D Amount        S                  9P 2
D Amountlen     S                  5u 0           Inz(%len(Amount))
D Array         S                  1              Dim(%len(Amount))
```

In this example, the variable Amountlen is initialized to nine, the length of the parameter Amount. The variable Array (an array) is defined with nine elements.

The %decpos BIF

The %decpos BIF analyzes the numeric parameter specified and returns the number of decimal positions of the numeric variable or expression. This BIF could be used as the parameter in the INZ keyword.

Here is an example:

```
D Amount          S              15P 5

D Amountdp        S               5u 0        Inz(%decpos(Amount))
```

In this example, the variable Amountdp is initialized to five, the number of decimal positions of the parameter Amount.

The %addr BIF

The %addr BIF returns the memory address of the variable specified as a parameter. This BIF could be used to set the initial value of a pointer variable, using the INZ keyword.

Here is an example:

```
D IndPtr          S               *           Inz(%addr(*IN))
```

The pointer variable IndPtr is initialized to the address of the indicator array, *IN. Indicators can now be accessed using the pointer.

The %paddr BIF

The %paddr BIF returns the procedure address pointer of the named procedure. This BIF could be used to set the initial value of a procedure pointer, by using the INZ keyword.

Here is an example:

```
D ExHandPgm     S               *           Procptr
D                                            Inz(%paddr('EXHANDLER'))
```

In this example, the procedure pointer ExHandPgm is initialized to the procedure address of program EXHANDLER. This is especially useful when calling IBM APIs.

The %elem BIF

The %elem BIF returns the number of elements of the named array, table, dimensioned data structure, or multi-occurrence data structure. This BIF could be used to set the initial value of a field using the INZ keyword, or the dimension size using the DIM keyword.

Here is an example:

```
D Array          S                 9p 2      Dim(200)

D NewArray       S                 5         Dim(%elem(Array))

D NumElem        S                 5u 0      Inz(%elem(Array)
```

In this example, the variable NewArray (an array) is defined with the same number of elements (200) as its parameter, Array. The variable NumElem is initialized to the value of the number of elements of array Array, which is 200.

BIFs in a Procedure, by Return Value

The BIFs in RPG IV can be categorized several ways. In Appendix B, for example, they are listed in alphabetical order. In this section, however, I have chosen to organize BIFs by their *return value*. A return value is a common function attribute. In this concept, the return value takes the place of the function after the function has performed its work. Some BIFs do not use a return value. These BIFs (discussed separately in a later section of this chapter) include those used for date manipulation, lists, and XML.

The Indicator Return Data Type

The indicator data type is a Boolean, defined with two values, zero and one. These values correspond identically to the values of named or numbered indicators as you have typically used them in your programs. These values are also known by their figurative constant names, *Off and *On. In hexadecimal, they have the values x'F0' and x'F1', and in EBCDIC, they are defined as character 0 and character 1.

Expressions used in conditional op-codes, such as If and Select/When, use an indicator data type (Boolean) as the result of the expression. Here is an example:

```
If  AmountDue > Payments;
```

In this case, if the AmountDue value is greater than Payments, then the expression is said to be "true," which translates to a value of one. If it *is not* true, then the expression translates to a value of zero. A BIF that returns an indicator data type can be used directly as the conditional expression, if you want to process on a true condition.

An assignment statement that has an indicator data type to the left of the equal sign will accept a BIF returning an indicator data type. Here is an example:

```
Sflend = %eof(datafile);
```

Many RPG IV built-in functions return a value of the indicator data type. Table 2.1 lists these BIFs.

Table 2.1: BIFs That Return Indicator Values	
%eof(filename)	This BIF returns *On if the read attempt reached end-of-file, beginning-of-file, or end-of-group (when using ReadE).
%equal()	This BIF returns *On when an exact match exists between the key argument of the prior SetII operation and the key of the file record where the file is currently positioned. This is a great way to verify the existence of a record without actually reading the record.
%error()	This BIF returns *On if two conditions are true. First, the previous operation must have specified the (e) op-code extender. Second, an exception must have occurred.
%found(filename)	This BIF returns *On if a record is found in the file whose key matches an argument on the previous Chain, SetII, Setgt, or Delete operations.
%nullind(field)	This BIF returns *On if the field named has a status of null.
%open(filename)	This BIF returns *On if the file named is currently open.
%shtdn	This BIF returns *On if the job where this program is running has received an End request.
%tlookup(arg:table:alt_table) Also: %tlookupgt() %tlookupge()%tlookuplt() %tlookuple()	This BIF returns *On if a table entry exists that meets the condition of the table lookup.

The Numeric Return Data Type

Many built-in functions return numeric values with different internal numeric data types. These BIFs are listed in Table 2.2.

Table 2.2: BIFs That Return Numeric Values	
%abs()	This BIF returns the absolute value of the numeric parameter.
%check()	This BIF returns an unsigned integer for the first position in a base string for a character that is not in a verification list.
%checkr()	This BIF returns an unsigned integer for the last position in a base string for a character that is not in a verification list.
%dec()	This BIF returns a packed decimal value from a numeric expression, character field, date, or time value.
%decpos()	This BIF returns an unsigned integer of the number of decimal positions defined for the parameter or expression.
%div()	This BIF returns a signed integer quotient of integer parameters.
%elem()	This BIF returns an unsigned integer of the number of elements (Dim value) of an array, data structure, or occurrences (Occurs value) for a multi-occurrence data structure.
%float()	This BIF returns the floating-point format of a numeric argument. This is important for passing parameters to programs written in C or Java.
%int()	This BIF returns a numeric value to integer format.
%len()	This BIF returns an unsigned integer of the length of a variable or literal, or it can set the current length of a varying length field.
%lookupxx()	This BIF returns an unsigned integer of the array index that meets the conditions specified in the parameters.
%occurs()	This BIF returns an unsigned integer of the current data structure occurrence. It can be used to set an occurrence.
%parms()	This BIF returns an unsigned integer of the number of parameters passed to a procedure.

Table 2.2: BIFs That Return Numeric Values *continued*	
%rem()	This BIF returns an unsigned integer of the remainder of the integer dividend and divisor parameters.
%scan()	This BIF returns an unsigned integer of the position of a search argument in a string.
%size()	This BIF returns an unsigned integer of the number of bytes in a variable, data structure, or literal.
%sqrt()	This BIF returns a packed decimal value of the square root of the numeric argument.
%uns()	This BIF returns an unsigned integer of the decimal or character expression parameter.
%xfoot()	This BIF returns a packed decimal sum of all elements of the array specified.

The Date, Time, and Timestamp Return Data Types

The date, time, and timestamp data types provide convenient ways to handle situations involving date and time computations. In free-format, we no longer have the TIME op-code that provided both the current time and the current date (from the system). These needs are now met using the %date and %time built-in functions. Table 2.3 lists the BIFs related to date and time.

Table 2.3: BIFs That Return Date, Time, and Timestamp Values	
%date()	This BIF returns a date data type, whose value depends on the parameters specified.
%time()	This BIF returns a time data type, whose value depends on the parameters specified.
%timestamp()	This BIF returns a timestamp data type from the character or numeric expression parameter.

The Character Return Data Type

Character fields are pretty common in the business world. The reference to
"string" in the term "character string" probably came from the C language,
where there are no character fields, just character arrays with a null (x'00') as
the last entry. The effect is a string of alphabetic characters with the null at
the end. RPG's character fields have a fixed or variable length, and no null.

There are BIFs for both character fields and character strings in RPG IV.
While most BIFs use the character field format, the term "character string"
is generally used to include BIFs for both character fields and character
strings. Table 2.4 lists character-field and character-string BIFs.

Table 2.4: BIFs That Return Character Values	
%char()	This BIF returns a character field from a numeric value or date/time/timestamp field.
%editc()	This BIF returns a character field of a numeric expression parameter with the application of the specified edit-code parameter.
%editflt()	This BIF returns a 23-byte character field that is the result of converting the numeric expression parameter to a printable floating-point format. This format is often called scientific notation.
%editw()	This BIF returns a character field of the numeric expression parameter with the application of the specified edit-word parameter.
%replace()	This BIF returns a character field using either character deletion, character insertion, or both.
%str()	This BIF returns a null-terminated character string from a character field, or conversely, it returns a character field from a character string.
%subst()	This BIF returns a character field of the portion of a specified character field at the specified starting location and length. This BIF can also be used on the left side of an assignment statement, to modify a character field at a specified location for a specified length.
%trim() %triml() %trimr()	This related set of BIFs returns either a character field with the removal of leading blanks (%triml), trailing blanks (%trimr), or both (%trim). In place of blanks, other characters can be specified.
%xlate()	This BIF returns a character field after a base value is inspected and possibly modified using translation patterns.

The Pointer Return Data Type

The pointer data type came into the RPG language in the mid-1990s, with the advent of RPG IV. Pointers in RPG IV are classified as either *basing pointers* or *procedure pointers*. Both kinds of pointers are specified with internal type of * (the asterisk) on definition specifications; however, a procedure pointer requires that the keyword PROCPTR be specified. Table 2.5 lists BIFs that return a pointer data type.

Table 2.5: BIFs That Return Pointer Values	
%alloc()	This BIF returns a basing pointer to allocated storage of the size specified in the parameter.
%realloc()	Like the %alloc BIF, this one also returns a basing pointer to storage. This BIF is used to make a previous allocation larger or smaller.
%addr(variable)	This BIF determines the storage address of the named variable and returns a basing pointer to the variable.
%paddr('procedure name')	The purpose of this BIF is to determine the address of the specified procedure name, and return a procedure pointer to it.
%this()	This BIF returns a procedure pointer to a procedure or method. It is used primarily for Java.

BIFs with No Return Values

Some BIFs serve highly useful purposes, but do not use the traditional return-value concept. These BIFs are listed in Table 2.6.

Table 2.6: BIFs with No Return Values	
Date and Time Arithmetic BIFs	
%years(value) %months(value) %days(value)	These three BIFs are used in date-arithmetic expressions, such as this one: New_Date = Old_Date + %years(3);
%hours(value) %minutes(value) %seconds(value) %mseconds(value)	These four BIFs are used in time-arithmetic expressions, such as this one: New_Time = time() + %hours(4) + %minutes(45);
List-type BIFs	
%fields(field1: field2:...)	This BIF is an option on the Update operation. Only the specified fields are updated.
%kds(key data structure: # of fields)	This BIF can be used on certain input/output operations to specify key arguments. Operations that might use this BIF include Chain, Setll, Setgt, ReadE, and ReadPE.
XML (Extensible Markup Language) BIFs	
%xml(xml-data: xml-options) oOr (xml-doc: xml-options)	This BIF returns the node/element indicated by the xml-options parameter, or returns all of the data.
%handler(subprocedure: first-parm)	This BIF identifies a subprocedure and the first parameter to pass to that subprocedure. This BIF is used with the %xml BIF to identify a subprocedure that the XML parser calls for each set of data retrieved from the XML document.

Summary

The new free-format RPG IV gives you the opportunity to use BIFs to perform essential tasks. Free-format RPG IV with BIFs is easy to code and even easier to maintain than the fixed-format scheme. There is even an option to use BIFs in definition specifications to help set up your fields, arrays, and data structures. In procedures, BIFs do much of the work in manipulating character and numeric data for you.

Using C Functions

Use library functions.
—Brian Kernighan and P.J. Plauger

M ost RPG programmers don't know the C programming language and avoid technical articles or discussions that have anything to do with it. Until 1993, so did I. That year, I took some college classes in which C was the only language that could be used for assignments. I found that C was very different from RPG, but writing my own functions was very appealing. When I returned to an RPG environment in 1994, I assumed that I would not see any C programming again. In late 1994, however, IBM introduced RPG IV and ILE. At that point, integrating C functions with RPG IV programs became a possibility.

Why Use C Functions?

The RPG IV language has a rich complement of op-codes and BIFs, so why would you consider accessing functions designed for the C language? The answer is that the C language gives you some functions you don't have in RPG, as well as functions that are more efficient than native RPG operations. Integrating C functions with your normal RPG code is easy, giving you the best of both languages.

To access a C function, you need to know the function's interface, including its name, number of parameters, parameter data types, and return value, if any.

To see why C functions might be useful to RPG programming, let's look at a few examples. Let's start with the C function Rand, which is used for random number generation. It has to be initialized with another function, called Srand, which "seeds" the random number generator. The notion of seeding is to set an initial value that is kept in the system somewhere. The Rand function cannot be used without first doing Srand, which must be run only once.

Here are a few technical details to keep in mind when using these functions:

- Srand requires an unsigned integer parameter, and there is no return value.

- Rand has no parameters, and returns an unsigned integer return value.

You'll see examples that use both the Rand and Srand C functions later in this chapter.

Now, let's look at another C function, Strtok. This function is called *string-token*, and it is a string parser. For example, consider the string "The cat is gray." This string can be broken into separate *tokens* of "The," "cat," "is," and "gray" by using this function repetitively.

Here are few technical details to keep in mind when using this function:

- Strtok requires a string parameter and a delimiter character.

- The return value for Strtok is a pointer to a token (a character string up to the first delimiter), or a null pointer.

- It is common practice to use a blank as the delimiter, but other characters can be used.

You'll find an example that uses the Strtok function later in the chapter.

Now, let's consider a higher math function, Sin (the trigonometric function sine). Here are few technical details to keep in mind when using this function:

- The Sin function has one parameter, the angle in radians.

- It must be defined as a floating-point data type, either 4f or 8f.

- The return value is also floating-point.

Review the IBM reference manual *ILE C/C ++ Runtime Library Functions Reference* for details on these or any other C function you might be interested in. The document number is SC41-5607. This IBM publication can be viewed on the web at the following link:

http://publib.boulder.ibm.com/infocenter/systems/scope/i5os/ topic/books/sc415607.pdf

How C Functions Work with RPG IV

Using a C function within an RPG IV program requires the use of a *prototype*. The prototype defines to RPG IV the function's return value (if any) and the parameters needed for the function.

For example, consider this use of the Sin function:

```
dsin                    pr              8f    extproc('sin')

d angle                                 8f    value
```

The prototype name is made the same as the C function. The return value definition of 8f is specified, and the external procedure name is specified ('sin'). On the second line, the name angle is optional, since names on prototype parameters are not required. The 8f is the definition of the parameter, and the keyword value is used, since parameters in C functions expect parameter passing by value.

The call interface is the same as for any external procedure. The CallP operation can be used if no return value is needed. The implicit call (which works just like a BIF) is used when the C function has a return value. As you will see throughout this book, the implicit call is emphasized as a preferred method.

Let's add a few more lines of code to the example above:

```
dSinans         s               8f

dAngleF         s               8f

dAngleP         s               7p 2    Inz(1.0456)

 /free

   AngleF = %float(AngleP);

   SinAns = sin(AngleF);
```

Three fields are defined:

- SinAns will hold the answer.

- AngleF is a floating-point work field.

- AngleP is the input angle, in packed-decimal format.

The first new line of code uses the %float BIF to convert the packed-decimal AngleP field to floating-point, and then assigns the value to the work field AngleF. The next line of code calls the function Sin implicitly, passing the work field AngleF as a parameter.

Random Numbers from C

One of the C functions that you might find useful is the random number function, mentioned earlier in this chapter. You'll see a detailed example using this function later, but for now, let me share the justification for using it in an application. The following situation occurred a couple of years ago:

I was working on an application to perform testing—giving an exam. The exam had four parts, with 10 questions in each part. The questions for each part came from a question pool, with 100 possible questions in the pool. The program needed to select, at random, 10 questions from each of the four associated question pools.

RPG IV does not have a random number function, but C does. Upon investigation, the Rand function in the C language was determined to be the proper choice. As explained earlier, Rand needs to be initialized by another C function, Srand.

The output from Rand is an integer between zero and 32,767. For the purposes of this application, I needed to scale that down to a range of zero to 99. A handy way to do this is to divide the return value by 100 (in this case), and use the remainder.

Because duplicate questions were not wanted in the exam, a check for a duplicate random number was needed, and duplicates discarded. The exam questions were stored in an array with indexes from one to 100, so the resulting random number needed to be incremented by one to match the RPG array index. Prototyping was needed for the two C functions, Rand and Srand, as follows:

```
D  Set_random          PR                     Extproc('srand')
D     Seed                        10u 0
D  Get_random          PR        10u 0        Extproc('rand')
```

Notice the use of the Extproc keyword, and the C function name in lower-case. This is required. For the Set_random prototype, there is no return value (the "seed" is stored somewhere in the system), but there is an un-signed integer requirement as the parameter. It is best to make this parameter as random as possible. I have found that using the micro-seconds value of the current timestamp is fairly random.

Also, ILE needs to locate the procedures rand and srand, so a binding directory needs to be specified on the H control specification. The H control specification must be placed first in the source member. Here is an example:

```
H       Bnddir('QC2LE')
```

Random number setup can be done as follows:

```
D Seed              S        10u 0
D Index             S        10i 0
 /free
   Dou Seed = 0;
      Seed = %subdt(%timestamp( ) : *MS);
      If Seed  0;
        Set_Random(Seed);
      Endif;
   Enddo;
    // Obtaining the random number,
    //  then scaling it to 0-99 is done as follow:
   index = Get_Random( );     // index 0-32767
   index = %rem(index:100);    // index 0-99
   index += 1;                // index 1-100
```

The code above sets the seed (in the Dou group), and then uses the random number function to set an index. The index is used to access an array element from a question pool. Additional programming is needed to avoid duplicate indexes. The index is used to access a question from a question array.

Checking for duplicate random numbers and further processing of the application is not shown here.

Occasionally, the need for higher mathematical functions comes up. This might involve the use of trigonometric functions such as sine, cosine, or tangent. These are not available in RPG IV, but all of them are available in C.

The following trig functions are available in C:

- **Acos** calculates the arc cosine.

- **Asin** calculates the arc sine.

- **Atan** calculates the arc tangent.

- **Atan2** is a variation of Atan() for calculating the arc tangent.

- **Cos** calculates the cosine.

- **Cosh** calculates the hyperbolic cosine.

- **Sin** calculates the sine.

- **Sinh** calculates the hyperbolic sine.

- **Tan** calculates the tangent.

- **Tanh** calculates the hyperbolic tangent.

Using the C run-time library functions and setting up the prototypes for C functions is an easy way to use features available in the C language.

C Data Types vs. RPG IV Data Types

The data types used by C functions are nearly all integer, float, and null-terminated strings. RPG IV supports all integer and float data types, and can convert null-terminal strings to RPG character fields, and vice versa (using the %str BIF). The integer and float data types available with

RPG IV make it easy to pass variable data back and forth between RPG IV and C.

One of the hurdles for RPG IV programmers is understanding the data types used by C, and matching them to RPG IV's scheme. Typically, RPG programmers have only used zoned or packed-decimal numeric fields. Table 3.1 describes how data types in the two languages relate to each other, including recommended RPG variable sizes.

Table 3.1: Most Common Data Types for C and RPG IV		
C Definition	**RPG IV Prototype Parameter Definition**	**Notes**
Int short	5i 0	Signed integer, two bytes
Int long	10i 0	Signed integer, four bytes
Unsigned int	5u 0	Unsigned integer, two bytes
Unsigned int long	10u 0	Unsigned integer, four bytes
Float	4f	Floating-point, standard precision
Double	8f	Floating-point, double precision
Char *	*	Defined in RPG with the VALUE and Options(*STRING) keywords
(*)	*	Defined in RPG with the VALUE and PROCPTR keywords

Parameter Passing to C Functions

When passing parameters to another procedure, RPG normally uses a technique called *passing by reference*, which means that a pointer address is used. In the called program, the parameter field is a template over the "passed" field in the calling program. If you modify the variable in the called program, you are really modifying the field in the calling procedure.

The C language uses a parameter passing technique called *passing by value*. In this scheme, the actual value of the parameter is passed. The value of the passed field can be changed in the called procedure, but the parameter field in the calling program is not changed. The RPG IV language can also pass parameters by value, simply by using the VALUE keyword for the parameter in the definition on the prototype.

A more flexible option is to use the keyword CONST instead of VALUE. This also passes parameters by value, but has some additional features. The CONST keyword allows you to use fields of different data types (for numeric data types) and lengths as a parameter (different than the prototype), including the use of a constant.

Character String Differences between C and RPG IV

The RPG IV language and C differ in their method of handling character strings. RPG IV uses fixed or varying-length character fields. The C language uses an array of a variable length, with the last entry in the array a null character (hex '00'). If you use the Options (*String) keyword on the parameter in the prototype for a character field, the compiler places the RPG IV character field specified into a work area, and then automatically adds the null character. The data in the work area is then passed to the C function.

Binding RPG IV and C Functions

After coding an RPG IV program with the proper prototypes, and using an implicit call to the C function using the prototype(s), there is still one more step to "glue" the pieces together. The C functions are in service programs known only to IBM, but IBM has given us access to these programs via binding directory QC2LE. By simply putting Bnddir('QC2LE') on the H control specification, the binder will locate and include the C functions you have requested.

You must also specify an activation group, but not the default activation group, since you are using ILE's binding by reference. While you are testing your new program, use *New as the activation group. This helps avoid testing problems. Otherwise, named activations stay around and are used on subsequent calls, even if you recompile and replace the program (as you will see in Chapter 5).

Here's an example of an H control specification:

```
H  Bnddir('QC2LE') Actgrp(*New)
```

This specifies that binding directory QC2LE be used during the binding phase, and that activation group *New be applied when the program is loaded and run. When you are past the testing phase, a named activation group might be your best alternative.

Using C Functions to Make Your Job Easier

I was asked to help with a data conversion, where the customer name in the "from" database was one big field, with spaces separating the parts of the name. In the "to" database, the name was divided into title, first name, middle initial, and last name fields. Other information about the "from" database included the following:

- Not every name had a title, but if a title existed, it was a standard title.

- A middle initial was optional, but if it existed, there was a period after it.

- Every character after the middle initial was part of the last name.

- If only one name appeared, it was the last name, not the first name.

Moving each part of the multi-part name field into the right new field became a programming project. It was accomplished completely in RPG IV, but a nagging inner voice kept saying to me, "This task could have been done more easily, somehow." After some research, I found a C function that could have helped: the Strtok (string token) function.

This is a parser-type function that helps in dividing portions of a character string. Something in the string has to be the delimiter, to tell the parser where one portion ends and the next begins. The C language calls these short string portions *tokens*. For example, using the Strtok function with the sentence "See Spot Run" and a space as the delimiter, you get "See" with one pass, "Spot" with a second pass, and "Run" with a third pass. This scheme would fit my data conversion situation pretty well, where blanks would be used to separate parts of the big name field. Of course, some logic would still need to be used to place each "token" item into its rightful place.

The Strtok Function

We'll review the most important elements of the new Strtok program in this section. (The entire program takes over a hundred lines of code, so it is not included here.) The field with the name to be parsed is FullName, defined 40A.

The first part of the main procedure is shown here:

```
h Bnddir('QC2LE') Actgrp(*New)

d GetToken           pr          *        ExtProc('strtok')

d   Name                         *        Value Options(*String)

d   Delimit                      *        Value Options(*String)
```

It has the H control specification with the IBM binding directory QC2LE specified, and the activation group *New. Following that is the prototype for the Strtok C function. The return value is a pointer to the found token, or a null pointer if no token is found. The two parameters are the field to be parsed and the delimiter.

The next section is a work array to hold all of the tokens, and a work field to hold the most current token:

```
d artok              s            like(FullName) dim(30)

d token              s            like(FullName)
```

The next few lines are work fields used in the procedure. The definition 5u 0 indicates an unsigned integer of five digits:

```
d ReturnAdr          s            *

d count              s            5u 0

d Space              c                    ' '
```

The count field defined here is used to count the number of tokens found, and used later in processing the token array elements.

The procedure begins by clearing the previous contents of the Title, FirstName, Initial, and LastName fields:

```
/free

   //* Clear output fields

   Clear Title;

   Clear FirstName;

   Clear Initial;

   Clear LastName;
```

The procedure continues by first checking for all-blank input. Next, it left-adjusts the FullName field, and then retrieves the first token from the FullName field:

```
   If FullName = *blank;

      //  Name is not all blank

      //  Shift Name to left, removing left blanks

      FullName = %triml(Fullname);

      ReturnAdr = GetToken(FullName:Space);
```

The function call GetToken here gets the first token. In the next section, GetToken gets the remaining tokens.

The next section is a loop to obtain and store the tokens of the FullName field:

```
Dow ReturnAdr <> *Null;   // Load Tokens into Artok array

   Token = %str(ReturnAdr);

   Count += 1;

   Artok(count) = %trim(Token);

   ReturnAdr = GetToken(*Null:Space);

Enddo;
```

Notice that the return value for the C function is a pointer to the token. The %str BIF takes the null-terminated string and moves the characters into a regular character-field-token. A count is made of how many tokens are saved in the array, to handle later processing. At this point, the tokens are stored in elements of the Artok array.

The use of the Strtok C function makes parsing the long FullName string very easy. The remainder of the program, not shown here, just puts the tokens in the correct output fields.

Exponentiation

There was a time when RPG could do little in the way of powers and roots. Powers were done by repetitive multiplications, and the only "root" capability was the square root. The use of C functions was the only solution for anything more complex. You might have done this.

It might seem contrary to bring this up in a chapter on using C functions, but the truth of the matter is that native RPG can now provide all you need in this mathematical arena.

With the advent of the ** (exponentiation) operator, all business formulas using an exponent can be done *without* using the C function library. In RPG IV, the exponentiation operator gives you the complete capability to determine the root or power of a number.

The form of an exponentiation operation is as follows:

```
Answer = number ** power;
```

In this formula, "power" can be a whole number, a fraction, or a mixed number. It can also have a negative sign.

Here are several examples of exponentiation, for your review:

```
/free

// Simple power and roots:

Area_Circle = 3.1416 * Radius ** 2;

//    The above computes the area of a circle using

//    the power 2

Cube_Root = 8 ** (1/3);

//    The above line computes the cube root of 8,

//    making Cube_root = 2.

Future_Val_Annuity = Period_Amt * (((1+i)**n-1)/i);

//    The above expression computes the future value

//    of an annuity. i is the periodic rate, and n

//    is the number of periods. With this formula, you can

//    determine how much money you will have if you save

//    Period_Amt for n periods at interest rate i.
```

As you can see, any formula needing exponents can be done without using C functions.

Summary

C functions provide capabilities that are useful to you, as an RPG IV programmer. In particular, if you have a math requirement needing the use of trigonometry or other higher mathematics, the appropriate C function will make the overall programming much easier. Other specialized C functions, such as the random number generator, are helpful for special projects.

The example of the Strtok C function in this chapter shows that combining C functions with native RPG operations enhances your overall programming toolset.

4

Subprocedures

Replace repetitive expressions by calls to a common function.
—Brian Kernighan and P. J. Plauger

RPG IV has an abundance of op-codes and BIFs, and a wonderful language feature that allows you to *write your own functions*. This feature is the ability to code subprocedures. Your subprocedures can take on many roles. For example, one could be a date-conversion routine, and another could compute state taxes. Writing your own functions makes your programming even more modular (and potentially reusable).

Comparing Subprocedures and Subroutines

Subprocedures and subroutines are similar, but also different. In RPG IV, subroutines are always part of the main procedure and can access all files, data structures, and fields defined in the main procedure. The access to any field in the main procedure is called *global visibility*.

A subprocedure may define files (in V6.1), data structures, and fields within the subprocedure. These data items are local to the subprocedure only. Data defined in the subprocedure uses automatic storage. This means that each time the subprocedure is called, storage is automatically allocated, and then deallocated when the subprocedure is exited. To keep the storage, the keyword Static can be used with its definition.

A subprocedure may access the global files, data structures, and fields of the main procedure if the subprocedure is appended to the main procedure source member. If the subprocedure is not part of the main procedure source member, access to variables outside the subprocedure is accomplished with parameter passing, return values, and the use of the import and export keywords on data structures, fields, and arrays.

Because a subprocedure can have a return value, you can make a subprocedure that interfaces with your main procedure just as a BIF does.

Comparing Subprocedures and Static-bound Modules

Subprocedures are called either directly using a prototype and the Callp operation code, or indirectly using the prototype name in an evaluation/assignment operation. The Callp op-code calls the subprocedure, but it does not support the concept of a return value.

A static-bound module is also called using a prototype and the Callp operation. Unlike the subprocedure, it cannot be called indirectly, since there is no capability for a return value.

A subprocedure, then, is most like a static-bound module with the added benefit that it can be called indirectly, and it has a return value.

The Anatomy of a Subprocedure

A subprocedure starts with a P specification, containing the subprocedure name and a "B" (for "begin"). If the subprocedure is to be called by another procedure, the Export keyword is needed on the "begin" procedure statement. As of V6.1 of the operating system, you may specify files after the P begin statement.

Following the file specifications are the definition specifications. The procedure interface is required. It is nearly identical to the prototype used by the calling program. The letters "PI" are used as the definition type, and the return value is defined by length and data type (if needed). Recall that a return value does not have a name.

Parameters follow the PI statement, just as with the PR. There is one major difference with the PI, however. On prototypes, parameters do not need to be named. On procedure interfaces, parameters *must* be named.

After the PI are additional definitions needed by the subprocedure. These can include data structures, arrays, and fields. These data items are "local" to the subprocedure. The main procedure cannot access them directly. If you are accessing file data from a file defined in the subprocedure, a data structure is required to contain the input data. No input or output specifications are generated by the compiler, as it is done in main procedures.

After the definition specifications are the calculations. To use free-format, you must specify the /free compiler directive, starting in position 7. Subprocedure calculations do not use the RPG cycle, so no LR indicator is needed. For subprocedures with a return value, the value is set with the Return operation and an expression. The expression can be a literal, a field, or a multi-field expression. The value determined by the expression becomes the return value. Again, remember that the return value of the subprocedure is not named, either here in the subprocedure or in the prototype. Depending on the logic of your subprocedure, you might have more than one Return statement.

A Typecheck Subprocedure

Here is an example of a subprocedure that receives a two-byte character field, and then checks two files to see if a record exists with a key equal to the two-byte character field:

```
P Typecheck        b

D Typecheck        pi           n

D   type                        2

   /free

      Setll type File2;    // File 2

      Setll type File3;    // File 3

   If %equal(File2) or %equal(File3);

      Return *On;

   Else;

      Return *Off;

   Endif;

   /end-free

 P typecheck           e
```

The subprocedure uses the two-byte field as an argument in a Setll operation to the two different files. If a record is not found in either file, a return
value of indicator data type is set to *Off. If a record match is found in either file, the return value is set to *On. Since this subprocedure needs to access two files, it would probably be coded within the source member
procedure, where the files are defined.

If you are using the V6.1 release of the i operating system, and the only
purpose of File2 and File3 is for verification, you may put the two file definitions in the subprocedure. It would look like this:

```
P typecheck          b

fFile2      if   e              k disk

fFile3      if   e              k disk

D typecheck          pi                 n

D  type                          2

 /free

  Setll type File2;      // File 2

  Setll type File3;      // File 3

  If %equal(File2) or %equal(File3);

    Return *On;

  Else;

    Return *Off;

  Endif;

 /end-free

 P typecheck          e
```

With this option, you can make the checking for "type" more generic, by
putting the subprocedure into a service program with other, similar
subprocedures.

Before continuing on with more examples, here are a few reminders for placing files in a subprocedure:

- Input and output specifications are not generated for files in a subprocedure. All input and output must be done with data structures.

- Files are automatically opened when the subprocedure is called, and they are automatically closed when the subprocedure ends (either normally or abnormally). You may also specify USROPN for a file, so its opening and closing can be controlled with Open and Close operations in the subprocedure.

- You can change the default opening and closing of the file (each time you invoke and leave the subprocedure) by specifying the STATIC keyword on the file definition specification. This means that the storage associated with the file (Open Data Path) is kept, and all invocations of the subprocedure will use the same file storage. If the file is open when the procedure returns, it will still be open on the next call to the procedure.

A Date-conversion Subprocedure

On the next page, there's another example of a subprocedure, this time to convert a six-digit decimal field, containing a date in month-day-year format to Long Julian format:

The subprocedure uses a six-digit decimal number as input, and returns a seven-digit decimal number in Long Julian format, which is composed of a four-digit year and a three-digit day-of-year. Since this routine is potentially needed in many programs, the Export keyword is specified. This keyword makes the subprocedure available to other programs that specify a correct prototype of this subprocedure and include a binding directory that includes the program where this subprocedure is located. This subprocedure will probably be placed in a service program with other date routines. (This "linking" is explained in more detail in Chapter 5, in the section on binding by reference.)

Another field is specified as a parameter in this subprocedure, to be feedback to the calling program. Its definition is character, and a value of one will be loaded in this field if there is a date-conversion error. In addition, if an error

occurs, the return value (the Long Julian date) is set to zero. This is a little re-
dundant, but allows for a valid return value, as well as an error flag.

```
P Date6toLJ          B                    Export
D                    pi           7s 0
D  Date6                          6s 0
D  Err                            1
  /free
    Monitor;
      Clear Err;
  /If Defined(*V5R3M0)
      Return  %dec(%date(Date6:*mdy):*longjul);
  /Else
      Return  %int(%char(%date(Date6:*MDY):*Longjul0));
  /Endif
        On-error *all;
          Err = '1';
        Return 0;
      Endmon;
  /end-free
P                    E
```

In this subprocedure, the /If Defined(*V5R3M0) compiler directive checks
the release level of the system. If it is V5R3M0, the return value is determined using the %dec and %date built-in functions. The %dec BIF was updated at that release level to convert a date data type to decimal. Prior to
this release, a more complex expression was required. This is shown above,
after the /Else statement. A Monitor/Endmon group is used to catch and
handle all date-conversion errors. On an error, the one-byte error field is set
to one, and the return value is set to zero.

If you are currently at V5R3M0 or higher, you can remove the three compiler directives (/If, /Else, and /Endif) and the second Return.

When converting a two-digit year to a four-digit year, keep the following restriction in mind: If the two-digit year is between 00 and 39, the resulting four-digit year is 2000–2039. If the two-digit year is between 40 and 99, the resulting four-digit year is 1940–1999. This algorithm is useful for the next 10 to 20 years, but eventually it will not be. During that time, I highly recommend converting stored dates to date data type, or some four-digit year format. (Many firms did this during the years approaching the year 2000.) You can always format a four-digit year as two digits on displayed or printed output.

The following program fragment shows how a calling program uses the Date6toLJ subprocedure:

```
H    Actgrp('ABC') Bnddir('DATEBD')

D Date6toLJ        PR              7 0

D  Date6                           6 0

D  Err                             1

D Julian           s              7 0

D Mydate           s              6 0

D Error            s              1

 /free

    --

    --

   Julian = Date6toLJ(mydate:Error);

   If Error <> *blank;

     // Handle invalid date here

   Else;

     // Use valid Julian date here

   Endif;
```

In this example, the H control specification shows that an activation group ABC is to be used at the run time for this program, and that a binding directory DATEBD can be used by the compiler at "bind" time to locate called procedures. The prototype for the subprocedure Date6toLJ is specified in the definition specifications, with a return value whose definition is packed decimal, with a length of seven, and zero decimal places. The prototype also specifies two parameters. The first is a packed-decimal parameter, defined with a length of six, and zero decimal places. The second is a character parameter, defined with a length of one. Work variables are used that match the prototype. The call to Date6toLJ is done implicitly, in the assignment expression.

Subprocedures within a Source Member

In some cases, a subprocedure can be placed in the same source member as the "main" procedure. The advantages of coding the subprocedure with the main source member are as follows:

- Simplicity. The subprocedure is "with" the procedure it is servicing. You don't have to look for it in another module.

- The subprocedure can access any of the main procedure's fields directly, without passing parameters or using the import and export keywords to gain access to them.

The main disadvantage of putting a subprocedure within the same source member as the main procedure is that you lose modularity. Other programs that need the function produced by the subprocedure must copy the subprocedure's source into their source member, duplicating it.

Here are a few additional points to remember when placing a subprocedure within a source member:

- The subprocedure must still be bound, so ILE must be used.

- The main procedure cannot access "local" fields of the subprocedure.

Figure 4.1 is an example screen for a program that takes an input character string and re-displays the string either left-adjusted, centered, or right-adjusted. The string management is done in subprocedures.

```
A                                      DSPSIZ(24 80 *DS3)
A                                      INDARA
A          R REC
A                                      CA03(03 'exit')
A                                   3 26'Left, Center, or Right Adjust'
A                                   5 11'Input String'
A            INPUTF       78A  B  7  2
A                                  10  1'Left'
A                                  10  6'Adjust:'
A            OUTL         78A  O 12  2
A                                  14  1'Center:'
A            OUTC         78A  O 16  2
A                                  18  1'Right'
A                                  18  7'Adjust:'
A            OUTR         78A  O 20  2
A                                  23 13'F3 = Exit'
```

Figure 4.1: This display file is used by a program that displays an input character string either left-adjusted, centered, or right-adjusted.

The input field's name is InputF. The left-adjusted output field's name is OutL, the centered output field is OutC, and the right-adjusted output field is OutR. Given that information, the following RPG IV program uses the display file in Figure 4.1 and three subprocedures to determine the three outputs:

```
FScreenstr cf   e           workstn      Indds(Inds)

D leftadj        pr          78

D  input78                   78          const

D center         pr          78

D  input78                   78          const

D rightadj       pr          78

D  input78                   78          const

D Inds           ds

D  exit                                  Overlay(Inds:3)

  /free

   dou exit;

     exfmt rec;

     if exit;

       leave;
```

```
                endif;
            outl = leftadj(inputf);
            outc = center(inputf);
            outr = rightadj(inputf);
         enddo;
         *inlr = *on;
        /end-free
       P LeftAdj          B
       D                  PI            78
       D Input78                        78              const
        /free
          Return %trim(Input78);
        /end-free
       P LeftAdj          E
       P Center           B
       D                  PI            78
       D Input78                        78              const
       D Work             S                             like(Input78)
       D  blks            S                      5u 0
         /free
           If Input78 = *blank;
             Return *blank;
           Else;
             Blks  = (%len(Work) - %len(%trim(Input78))) / 2;
             %subst(Work:blks+1:%len(%trim(Input78))) =
                 %subst(%trim(Input78):1:%len(%trim(Input78)));
             Return Work;
           Endif;
          /end-free
       P Center           E
       P Rightadj         B
       D                  PI            78
```

```
D Input78                       78        const
D work              S                     like(Input78)
  /free
    Evalr Work = %trim(Input78);
    return Work;
  /end-free
P                   E
```

Figure 4.2 is an example of the screen at run time, showing the three outputs that first left-adjust a string, then center it, and then right-adjust it. All three subprocedures for adjusting the string are coded within the main program source member.

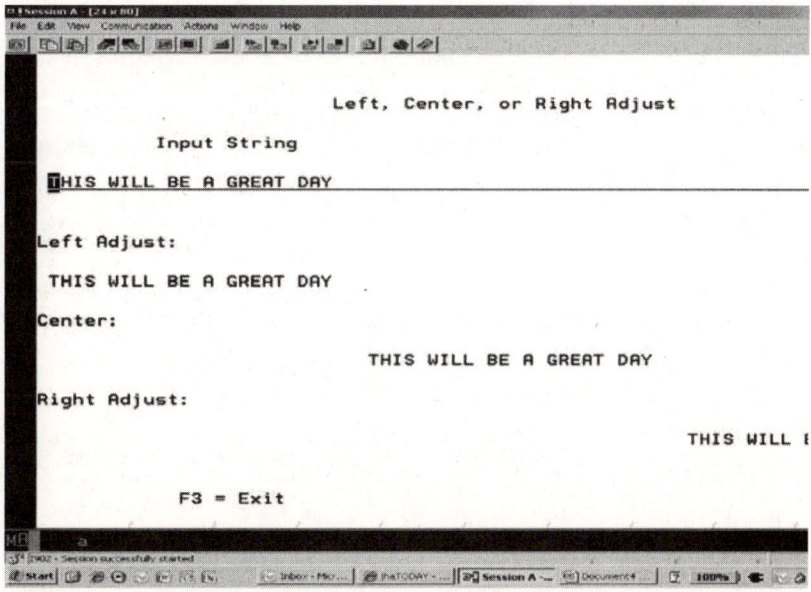

Figure 4.2: This panel displays the results of running the example program that invokes each of the three subprocedures.

Subprocedures outside of a Source Member

Using ILE's capabilities, the subprocedures in the previous example can be removed from the source member of the main procedure, yet still be available to the main procedure. In effect, you make the subprocedures available to any procedure that sets up the procedure interface (the prototype) properly. The advantages of coding the subprocedures separately are as follows:

- The subprocedures become available to any procedure, which is similar to the way a BIF works. This makes your code highly modular.

- While fields in the main procedure are not automatically available, the procedure interface can include many parameters. Also, the keywords import and export can be used to access main procedure data items.

Here are some points to remember when coding subprocedures outside the main procedure:

- In this method, a subprocedure must be exported to be available to any calling procedure.

- The main procedure cannot access the local variables of the subprocedure.

- Subprocedures are usually put in a source member with the NOMAIN control spec keyword. Prototypes for the subprocedures are needed in the source member for both the main procedure and the NOMAIN member.

Using the example program from the previous section, the three subprocedures are placed in a separate NOMAIN module (named "MODLCR") as follows:

```
H Nomain
D leftadj          pr                78
D  input78                           78        const
D center           pr                78
D  input78                           78        const
D rightadj         pr                78
D  input78                           78        const
P LeftAdj          B                           export
D                PI                  78
D Input78                            78        const
```

```
      /free
          Return %trim(Input78);
      /end-free
 P LeftAdj       E
 P Center        B                        export
 D               PI            78
 D Input78                     78         const
 D Work          s                        like(Input78)
 D blks          s             5u 0
      /free
         If Input78 = *blank;
            Return *blank;
         Else;
           Blks  = (%len(Work) - %len(%trim(Input78))) / 2;
           %subst(Work:blks+1:%len(%trim(Input78))) =
              %subst(%trim(Input78):1:%len(%trim(Input78)));
           Return Work;
         Endif;
      /end-free
 P Center        E
 P Rightadj      B                        export
 D               pi            78
 D Input78                     78         const
 D work          s                        like(Input78)
  /free
    Evalr Work = %trim(Input78);
    Return Work;
  /end-free
 P               E
```

This module is compiled with PDM option 15 (Create Module).

The main procedure now does not have the subprocedure source. To get to the subprocedures at run time, a binding directory (LCR) is used. Here is the main procedure, as modified:

```
H bnddir('LCR')

Fscreenstr      cf   e              workstn   Indds(Inds)

D leftadj            pr             78

D   input78                         78          const

D center             pr             78

D   input78                         78          const

D rightadj           pr             78

D   input78                         78          const

D   Inds             ds

D    exit                                       Overlay(Inds:3)
 /free
   dou exit;
     exfmt rec;
     if exit;
        leave;
     endif;
     outl = leftadj(inputf);
     outc = center(inputf);
     outr = rightadj(inputf);
   enddo;
   *inlr = *on;
```

A service program is created, called LCR, with module MODLCR as its only component. The binding directory LCR is also created, specifying the MODLCR service program as its only component. Then, the above program is compiled, using PDM option 14 and activation group *New.

Summary

In the previous two examples, the subprocedures LeftAdj, Center, and RightAdj are used in the main procedure. By using the return-value concept and an implicit call, these "homemade" functions are as easy to include in programs as any BIF.

By organizing your own functions into service programs, and using a binding directory to reference them, you enhance your productivity and make it easier to accomplish your programming goals. Documenting your subprocedures is part of the job, too, even if it seems like drudgery. When a new person needs to change or correct programs that use your functions, the documentation will prove valuable.

Using Prototyping and ILE
to Connect the Functional Parts

Write and test a big program in small pieces.
—Brian Kernighan and P. J. Plauger

I LE, the Integrated Language Environment, is essential in a modular, functional style of programming. This chapter describes prototyping, the procedure interface, binding (by copy and by reference), the service program, and binding directories. Since many API programs are "bindable," the last section of this chapter describes how to integrate APIs into your program.

Prototyping

A main procedure must use a prototype in its definition specifications, whether calling a procedure directly or indirectly. If the called procedure is a subprocedure or a bound module, prototyping and ILE methods must be followed to complete addressability to all of its components.

A prototype is a generic definition of the interface to a called procedure. Prior to RPG IV, this interface was accomplished with a parameter list. Parameters were passed by reference (only). With a prototype, you now have a wide range of options in passing parameters.

Let's first consider a prototype that simply replaces a dynamic call. Until binding came along in ILE RPG IV, the dynamic call was all we had in RPG. It is still very much in use today.

Here is a dynamic call in RPG IV, using a parameter list:

```
C                   Call    'EX0201'

C                           Parm            Compno   20

C                           Parm            Custno   70
```

Note that only fixed-format can be described here, since free-format does not have the CALL or PARM operations defined.

Here is the same dynamic call as the previous example, but in free-format RPG IV:

```
D Pgm2            PR                  Extpgm ('EX0201')

D   Parm1                  2 0

D   Parm2                  7 0

  /free

    CallP     Pgm2(compno: custno);
```

In this case, a prototype definition is required. The prototype name does not need to be the same name as the procedure being called, but sometimes that is done to increase clarity. Also, the naming of the parameters, Parm1 and Parm2 in this case, is optional. The parameter definitions, however, are required.

Here are some additional things to note about this call:

- The CallP (Call with Prototype) is used for dynamic calls. It can also be used for bound calls if no return value is needed.

- The prototype name is used on a CallP, followed by the parameters being passed.

- The variables being passed (compno and custno) must match the prototype, by position and data type. Usually, the variables will also match the prototype by length, but they don't have to, if certain keywords are provided on the prototype (such as Const). These variables are defined elsewhere in the program.

- A colon is used to separate multiple parameters.

Now, let's look at the called program to see what the differences are between the fixed-format and free-format methods. In the following example, the fixed-format *Entry PLIST is shown, for the called program EX0201:

```
C     *Entry          PLIST
C                     PARM                    Co        20
C                     PARM                    Cust      70
```

Since this example uses parameter passing by reference, the fields Co and Cust will assume the addresses of the passing variables, Compno and Custno. If Compno has a value of 25, then Co will be 25. If you modify a passed variable, you are also modifying the variables in the calling program.

The free-format variation must include both a prototype and a procedure interface. Neither PLIST nor PARM are available in free-format:

```
D EX0201          PR
D  Parm1                                      2 0
D  Parm2                                      7 0
D EX0201          PI
D  Co                                         2 0
D  Cust                                       7 0
 /free
    // Fields Co and Cust are available now
```

When reviewing this code, note the following:

- Inside the called program, the name on the prototype and the procedure interface (PI) should be the same, and match the procedure name.

- The names "Parm1" and "Parm2" in the prototype are optional, just as before.

- Parameter names after the PI are necessary and comparable to the PARM lines used in fixed format.

- The prototype and procedure interface do all of the parameter-passing work. (You'll learn more about the procedure interface in the next section of this chapter.)

- The keyword EXTPGM and its parameter are not needed in the prototype in the called program.

The Procedure Interface

A procedure interface is defined in procedures (or programs) that are called. There are a few differences between a procedure interface and the prototype that is used to define the procedure to the calling program. First, the procedure interface is defined with a PI instead of a PR. On a procedure interface, the parameters must be named. These names correspond by position to the parameters being passed by the calling program. Parameter names are not required in a prototype, but can be used as documentation.

Parameter passing is done by reference (address), unless specified otherwise. This means that in the called program, any use of a passed parameter is the same as using the corresponding variable in the calling procedure. To avoid modifying a variable being passed, use the keyword Const or Value. (These keywords and others are discussed later in this chapter.)

Now that you have some understanding of prototyping and the procedure interface, let's expand their use in calling modules or subprocedures. In both cases, ILE methods are employed. Details on ILE binding are discussed later in this chapter. For now, just the prototype and procedure interface are described.

Chapter 4 included an example of converting a six-digit decimal date in MMDDYY format to a seven-digit Long Julian format. Let's say that you want a variation of this, so that the two-digit years 00 through 49 convert to the four-digit years 2000 through 2049. IBM's date conversion turns two-digit years 40 and higher into 19*xx*.

A coworker tells you that this conversion routine has already been done, and you can use the subprocedure DATCV67. It requires the six-digit date as a parameter and has the seven-digit Long Julian value as a return value. Here is how you could code a program to use the subprocedure that is already completed and available:

```
D  Indate            S        6  0     Inz (070709)

D  LJulian           S        7  0

D  Date_conv         PR       7  0     Extproc('DATCV67')

D    date_parm                6  0

 /free

   - - -

     LJulian = Date_conv(Indate);

   - -
```

Since this prototype specifies an external procedure, an ILE activation group must be specified. Since the subprocedure is probably part of a service program, a binding directory will probably be specified in the program's H control specification. (You'll see examples of specifying binding directories and activation groups later in this chapter.)

The next example calls another program to provide a string-replace function. Assume you have a main 40-byte character string, a search string, and a replacement string. The idea is that if the search string is found in the main string, it will be replaced by the replacement string. This find-and-replace is to be repeated for the entire main string. The replacement string can be shorter or longer than the search string. Right-side truncation will be allowed without error.

A program module named SCANREPL is found that performs this function. It is already compiled and available as a *MODULE object. The parameter list requires the input string, the scan string (a maximum of five characters), the replacement string (again, a maximum of five characters), and an output character string, the same size as the input string.

Here is the code to perform the search, using the available SCANREPL module:

```
D   main_str             S          40
D   search_str           S           5
D   replace_str          S           5
D   output_str           S                     Like(main_str)
D Replace                PR                     Extproc('SCANREPL')
D   input                           40
D   scan-str                         5
D   repl-str                         5
D   output                          40
 /free

    CallP   Replace(main_str:search_str:replace_str:

                     output_str);
```

Since the prototype did not define a return value, CallP (the explicit call) must be used. ILE methods must be used, including an activation group, and (probably) a binding directory on the program's H control specification.

Prototype/Procedure Interface Keywords

Parameter passing has some flexibility in prototyped calls that is not available in fixed-format calls. Various keywords are available for parameters specified on a prototype and procedure interface. The following sections summarize the parameter-passing keywords available for prototypes.

Value

The Value keyword tells the compiler that you want the value of the variable to be sent to the called procedure. By using this option, the called procedure gets the information it needs, but it cannot change the value in the calling program.

The traditional RPG parameter-passing method is by reference, which means that the address of the variable in the calling program is sent to the called program. If the called program modifies the passed parameter, it is being changed in the calling program. The storage for the variable is defined in the calling program. Using Value in the procedure interface of the called program tells the compiler to allocate storage for the parameter. When the program is called, the value from the calling program is placed in the parameter's storage. Any updates to the variable are local to the called program.

Const

The Const keyword on a prototype parameter provides several capabilities. Similar to Value, the called program may treat the parameter as read-only if the Const keyword is also used on the procedure interface. If the called program does not use Const in the procedure interface to match this parameter, and the variable used in the CallP matches the prototype by numeric type and size, the called program can change the parameter's value. In addition, the compiler will generate temporary fields to accommodate mismatches in parameter length, numeric data type, or both, to accommodate differences between the prototype and the variable (or expression) used on the CallP. This eliminates the need for programmers to make up work fields to use on the CallP.

Options(*NoPass)

The *NoPass option on a parameter means that this parameter is optional; that is, it does not have to appear on the parameter list of the call. If *NoPass is specified for a parameter, then all parameters that follow it must also specify *NoPass.

Options(*Omit)

The *Omit option can be used on a parameter that is not required, but happens to fall in the middle of a parameter list. To actually omit the parameter in the call, specify *Omit in the parameter list where this parameter would normally be placed.

To determine whether the parameter was actually passed, in the called program, check the address of the parameter (using the %addr BIF) to see if it is equal to null. If it is, the parameter was omitted. If the parameter was omitted, any attempt to use it in the called program will result in a run-time error.

The *Omit keyword can be specified in addition to the Const keyword.

Options(*Varsize)

The *Varsize option in the prototype allows a character parameter to be shorter than the prototype value. (No option or keyword is needed for a character parameter to be longer than the prototype value). When using the *Varsize option, the called program or procedure must determine how many characters were actually sent. This can be done with another parameter containing the length. This option is only available when passing parameters by reference.

Options(*String)

The *String option in the prototype is used with basing pointer parameters. A pointer can be specified in the parameter list of the call, or a character expression can be used. If a character expression is used, a null (x'00') is placed at the end of the character expression. This option would be used primarily when calling procedures written in C.

Options(*RightAdj)

When the *RightAdj option is used on a prototype parameter, either the Const or Value keyword must also be specified. The character parameter value will then be right-adjusted in the parameter field.

Options(*Trim)

When the *Trim option is specified on a prototype parameter, either the Const or Value keyword must also be specified. The character type parameter value will be passed (using a temporary work field) without leading or trailing blanks. If the *RightAdj option is also specified, the parameter will be padded on the left with blanks. If the *RightAdj option is not specified, the parameter will be padded on the right with blanks. If the character parameter has a varying length, only the non-blank characters are passed.

Binding to Make "Modular" Work Efficiently

Binding is an ILE concept. For the i operating system, using RPG IV (and other programming languages), two forms of static binding are available. Static binding determines and sets procedure addresses in a program object. This step can be accomplished using the CRTPGM command, or by using the combined Compile and Then Bind command, CRTBNDRPG. If you are using PDM (the Program Development Manager), CRTBNDRPG is option 14.

Binding requires knowledge of modules and procedures. These are supplied to CRTPGM via parameters. For CRTBNDRPG, the module and procedure information can be supplied by referencing a binding directory.

Bind-by-Copy

The simplest form of binding is called *bind-by-copy*. In this method, all
modules to be called by the main procedure, and the main procedure itself,
are compiled using the command CRTRPGMOD (Create RPG Module),
PDM option 15. The CRTPGM command is then used to combine the modules into a program. Using another method, the non-main modules can be
created separately using CRTRPGMOD, and then the main procedure can be
compiled with CRTBNDRPG (option 14) using a binding directory.

A module is saved as an object of type *MODULE. Modules are not programs and cannot be called. Figure 5.1 is a diagram of the bind-by-copy
method.

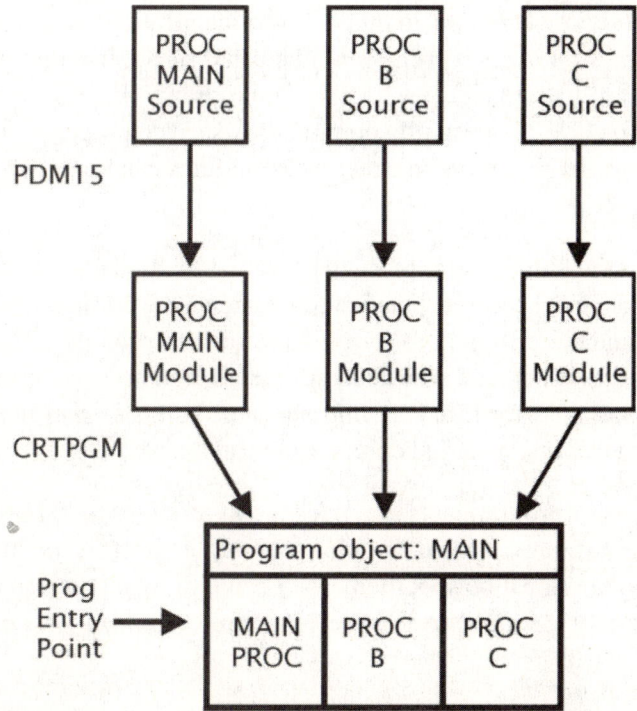

Figure 5.1: This diagram shows the bind-by-copy method, with a MAIN module that calls
modules PROCB and/or PROCC. It is also possible that PROCB calls PROCC.

Figure 5.1 shows that a program entry point, or PEP, needs to be set. The PEP is the module where the program is to start. In this case, it's MAIN. A copy of each module is part of the loadable program.

MAIN contains bound calls to PROCB and PROCC, by use of prototypes and the keyword EXTPROC. Both PROCB and PROCC have prototypes and procedure interfaces. These three source members can be compiled (option 15) with "loose ends" as a part of the *MODULE object.

MAIN needs to have the addresses of PROCB and PROCC determined. The parameters of the call(s) are "loose ends" also. During bind-by-copy, the procedure addresses of PROCB and PROCC are provided to MAIN, and the parameter addresses in MAIN are provided to modules PROCB and PROCC. Addressability is completed, allowing inter-module "calls" to be very fast, compared to dynamic calls.

Bind-by-Reference

In the *bind-by-reference* method, a service program object is used. A *service program* is not a program in the usual sense. It cannot be loaded and run as program objects are. A service program is a repository of modules that have been successfully compiled. A service program might contain only two or three modules, but these modules can contain many subprocedures.

A common practice is to place many (eight to 10) subprocedures in a source module. The H control specification contains the OPTIONS(*NOMAIN) keyword, and the main part of the module contains prototypes for the subprocedures. There are no calculations at all, and no program cycle, and no setting of indicator LR. The subprocedures in this scenario must have the Export keyword specified on the Begin statement.

The service program acts as a package of modules or subprocedures for the main procedures. When a service program is created, the modules that it will contain must be specified. They can either be typed as parameters to the CRTSRVPGM (Create Service Program) command, or a binding directory can be used.

Figure 5.2 shows the elements of the bind-by-reference method. The program MAIN calls PROCB and the subprocedures MATH and CENTERL. The subprocedure DATEX is in the service program BD, but is not used by the program MAIN.

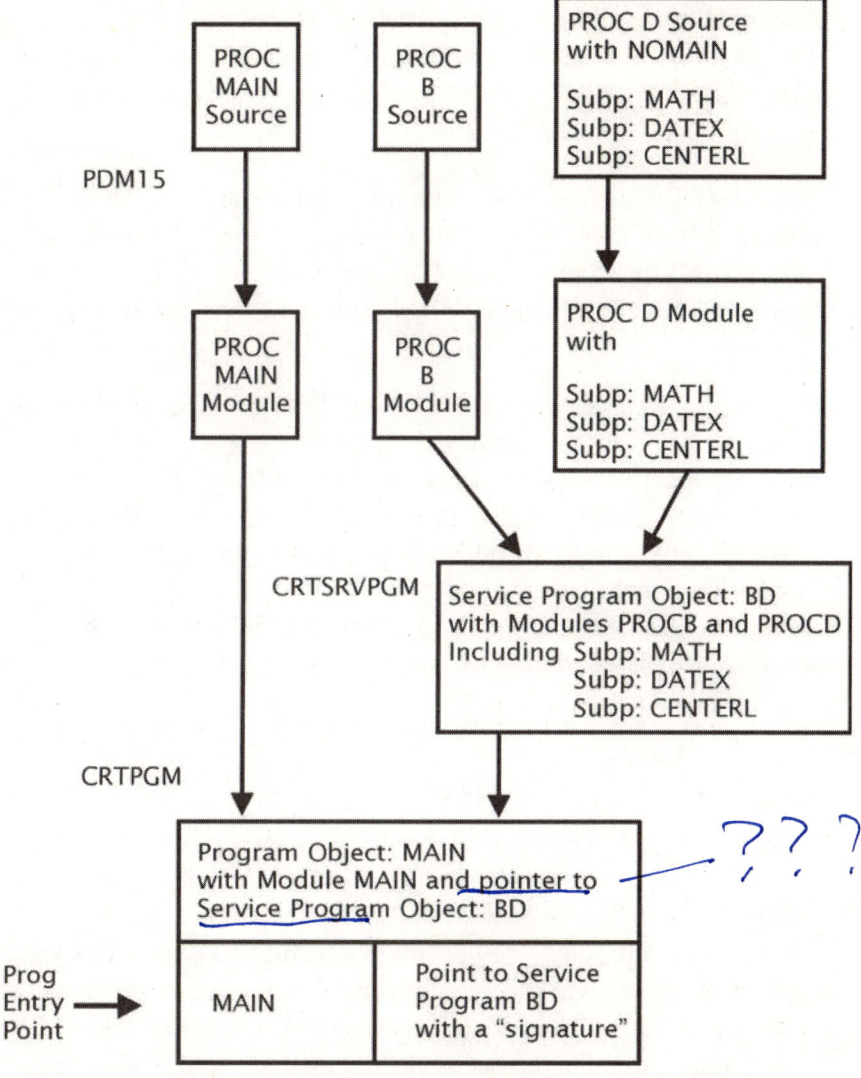

Figure 5.2: This diagram shows the bind-by-reference method, with the MAIN module calling module PROCB and subprocedures MATH and CENTERL. The service program BD includes a subprocedure DATEX not used in this program.

At program load time, the MAIN procedure of the program is loaded. Then, the pointer to the service program is used to load the procedures MATH, DATEX, and CENTERL. Although DATEX is not used, it is still loaded. After all modules are loaded, the program may run.

Comparing Bind-by-Copy with Bind-by-Reference

Bind-by-copy is noticeably simpler to implement than bind-by-reference. It also has a great performance impact over dynamic calls. It has one small disadvantage, however.

Modules used to create a program may be used again to create a different program. If a component module needs to be changed, then after the module is built, all programs that use this module must be updated (with UPDPGM) or rebuilt (with CRTPGM). Tools must be used to keep track of where component modules are used.

The bind-by-reference method has more activities and parts to it, and it also provides excellent performance. The biggest advantage in bind-by-reference is that few tasks need to be done when a component module of a service program needs to be changed. After the source is changed and compiled (a *MODULE is created), the service program that includes this component must be updated (with UPDSRVPGM). That's all! The programs that reference the changed module via the service program do not have to be updated or modified in any way.

Service programs can be organized to have modules and/or subprocedures of similar functionality. For example, you could have a "date management" service program, a "string management" service program, or an "edit routines" service program.

The Service Program Signature

One of the features of a service program is the *signature*. A signature is somewhat like a level check used with files. A level check occurs when a file is changed after it is used to compile a program with that file. When you call the program, the operating system discerns a difference in the file and issues the level-check error.

When you create a program using a service program as input for procedures, the service program provides a signature. At run time, the saved signature in the program is compared to the current signature(s) in the service program, retrieved at program load time. If a match is found, all is well, and the program runs. If no match is found, a signature error is issued, and the program does not run.

A signature is formulated from the procedure names comprising the service program, and their order. It can also be specified using binder language.

Multiple signatures are possible, allowing a minimal impact to program rebuilding.

Here's how it works:

Suppose you build a service program with two procedures, called PROCA and PROCB. You then build several programs using this service program. Eventually, you want to add two additional procedures (PROCC and PROCD) to the service program. You build the service program with four procedures.

Because you know this will change the signature of the service program, you use parameter Export on the CRTSRVPGM to provide "binder source" information. The source file member specified is not compiled. It is used by the service program creator to provide multiple signatures in the service program. The term used by the binder source is *previous or *current. You can have many sets of *previous, but only one *current.

The binder source for this example is as follows:

```
STRPGMEXP       Type(*current)

Export              Symbol(procA)

Export              Symbol(procB)

Export              Symbol(procC)

Export              Symbol(procD)

ENDPGMEXP

STRPGMEXP       Type(*previous)

Export              Symbol(procA)

Export              Symbol(procB)

ENDPGMEXP
```

Each group starting with STRPGMEXP and ending with ENDPGMEXP creates a signature of the procedures, including their order. By having a signature that matches the earlier two-procedure service program, the programs that were created with a service program with two modules do not have to be re-created.

Making up multiple signatures as the service program grows allows for minimal impact to program re-creation. At some point, there are very few changes to a service program, and it might be prudent to reset the service program back to just one signature (with all the modules), and then re-create all the programs that use the service program. Various source documentation aids on the market can help you find out where a service program is used.

The Binding Directory

I've mentioned the use of a binding directory several times in this chapter. This section explains what a binding directory is and how it is used.

A binding directory is an object (type *BNDDIR) that contains reference information about modules, service programs, or both. It is used by the Create Service Program command to locate the modules used in the service program. The only alternative is to carefully type the module information as parameters to the CRTSRVPGM command.

A binding directory is also a great help when creating programs. The keyword BNDDIR is available on the H control specification in RPG IV, so the binder will know where modules and service programs are during the binding phase. Again, the only alternative is to carefully type the module and service program information as parameters on the CRTBNDRPG command. Another benefit is having fewer steps in the program build process.

In the discussion of C functions in Chapter 3, binding directory QC2LE was mentioned. This binding directory, provided by IBM, provides all the information needed by the binder when using C functions.

You will want to create some binding directories that reference the modules and service programs you create for modularizing your applications. When documenting your subprocedures, specify the binding directory needed to allow access to the subprocedure at program bind time.

Here is an example of creating a binding directory:

```
CRTBNDDIR  BNDDIR(PRLIB/PRBDIR)
```

Now, an "empty" binding directory named PRBDIR exists in library PRLIB.

Next, modules and service programs are added to the binding directory:

```
ADDBNDDIRE   BNDDIR(PRLIB/PRBDIR) +

     MODULE(USTAX)                        +

     SRVPGM(STATETAX)
```

After running this command, two entries exist in binding directory PRBDIR. The first entry is for module USTAX, and the second entry is for service program STATETAX.

API Interfacing

IBM's APIs (Application Program Interfac*es*) are programs written by IBM that provide many valuable functions that RPG IV does not supply. Many books written by IBM and other authors describe the available APIs. This section describes how to set up your RPG IV programs to interface to the various APIs.

Dynamic Calls

Older APIs are called the traditional way, using a dynamic call. Earlier in this chapter, the prototype for a dynamic call was described. The following is an example of calling IBM's API QCMDEXC. This API allows an RPG program to run a command.

Here is the prototype and sample call:

```
  * Protyped call for QCMDEXC ----------------
D  CMDEXC              pr                    extpgm('QCMDEXC')
D  Cmdline                       1024A       Options(*Varsize) Const
D  CmdLen                        15P 5       Const
D  MsgText             S         50
  /free
    MsgText = 'This is a test';
    CmdLine = 'SNDMSG MSG('''   + %trim(MSGTXT) +
                     ''')   TOMSGQ(MYMSGQ)  ';
    Callp(e)  CMDEXC(Cmdline : %size(Cmdline));
```

In addition to being accessible the dynamic way, many newer APIs are also bindable. These APIs are procedures that can be bound to your programs. Higher performance can be expected for repeated calls to these procedures.

A good example of a bindable API is the use of an exception handler. An exception handler can be very useful in program error management. For example, consider the use of math in EVAL expressions. When RPG IV became available, math in EVAL expressions became commonplace. A slight difference occurs in RPG IV with EVAL, compared to the older math op-codes. If a numeric field overflows (because it is set to a value greater than its defined length), the older math op-codes ignore the condition. The new EVAL operation does not ignore the condition. Instead, an overflow exception is sent to the program.

The overflow condition may indicate a "bug," but it may also be fine, and the right thing to do is to ignore the exception. Ignoring an overflow exception is not possible using traditional methods. EVAL does not permit the (e) error op-code extender. Allowing the *PSSR subroutine won't work, either, since error recovery from a global error is not possible.

The use of the bindable APIs CEEHDLR and CEEHDLU solves this problem. The API CEEHDLR registers (enables) an exception-handling program that you write. Whenever any exception comes to your program, the exception-handling program is called, automatically. In your exception-handling program, you check for exceptions specific to numeric overflow. If true, the program can resume with no error message. If the exception is not overflow, you percolate (resume the error) back to the program and take the error "hit" as usual.

Here is an example of the prototype for calling the bindable API CEEHDLR:

```
D CEEHDLR           pr                      extproc('CEEHDLR')
D                                  *        Procptr
D                                 10
D                                  1        Options(*Omit)
```

Here are the other items needed in the program:

```
D pIgnore         s          *              procptr
D                                           inz(%paddr('IGNM'))
D               sds
D ProgName       *proc
 /free
   // Calling the API to enable the exception handler
      CallP Ceehdlr(pIgnore:ProgName:*omit);
   // The program IGNM is called when an exception
   //  occurs. It is up to this program to either
   //  ignore the error or allow it to percolate.
```

Activation Groups

Many people have called an activation group a smaller unit of work than a job, and within a job. I like to think of an activation group as a container for resource management and memory for program storage. I like pictures and diagrams, so my version of this definition is shown in Figure 5.3.

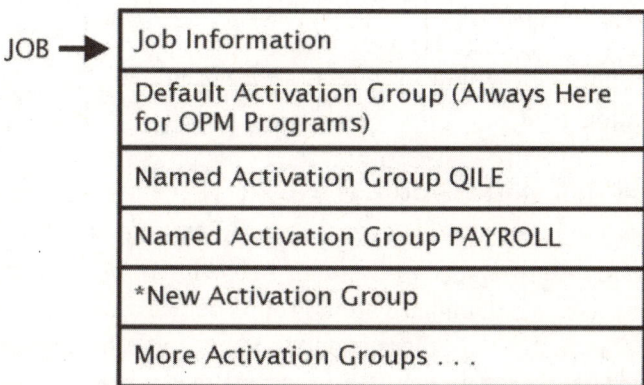

Figure 5.3: This diagram illustrates the division of a job that uses activation groups.

Activation groups have storage (dynamic and static) for program variables needed at program activation time. They also have a place to store resource factors, such as file overrides. An activation group is something like a container that compartmentalizes the application execution. It also protects resources from programs in the same job, but in different activation groups. This maintains resource integrity.

Packaged software can run independently in its own activation group, and not affect programs running in other activation groups. And when it comes to overrides, there is no longer dependence on the invocation stack. An override can be "scoped" to an activation group, the traditional calling stack scheme, or even the entire job.

Storage is allocated to the activation group when it is "activated." This simply means that if the activation group named in a program does not currently exist when the program is called (activated), the activation group is created, and the needed requirements for storage and resource management are allocated. If more requirements come along for the same activation group, the storage allocation is made larger.

The activation group stays in the job until one of the following occurs:

- It is removed by overt actions (with command RCLACTGRP, for example).

- An unhandled exception occurs.

- The job ends.

When the activation group ends, all storage attributed to the activation group is released.

The following sections provide brief descriptions of the different kinds of activation groups.

The Default Activation Group

The default activation group was designed to run non-ILE programs. These programs are often called *Original Program Model* (*OPM*) programs. There are two default activation groups per job, but the system uses one of these. So, in practice, there is only one per job. The designers of the operating system did not expect ILE programs to run here, but it is possible. IBM does not recommend that you do this, however, since storage used by ILE programs cannot be released.

When you are creating programs that include subprocedures, or prototypes to external procedures, the binder will not allow you to specify the default activation group. ILE programs end up here (again, not a good practice) by specifying an activation group of *Caller. Then, the program is called from a program that is running in the default activation group.

The default activation group exists for the life of the job, and cannot be reclaimed.

The Named Activation Group

The name for a named activation group is specified on the CRTPGM, CRTSRVPGM, or CRTBNDRPG command, or on the H control specifications (keyword ACTGRP) of an RPG IV program.

Here is an example:

```
H    Actgrp('QILE')
```

This activation group is created when the program is called, and the named activation group is not currently in the job. This activation group is *persistent* in that it stays in the job until it is destroyed via the RCLACTGRP command or end-of-job, or until the API CEETREC is run. Programs written in RPG IV and CL that end do not cause the named activation group to end.

This persistence feature has additional qualities. When a program is run in this activation group, and then ends (even with indicator LR turned on), the program and the storage for the program are *not* removed from the activation group. If you call the program again in the same job, the system will determine that it already has a copy in memory (in the activation group), and run it again. The initialization of variables is done, and files are opened as usual. Overall, this is a performance enhancer.

During the testing of new programs, however, this feature becomes an aggravation. We are all used to finding a bug, fixing it, and then re-running the program. With program persistence, the system will call the prior version of the program (the one with the error) and the bug fix will not be there! To remove the old copy, you must reclaim the activation group before you call the latest iteration of your program. With the named activation group gone, the system is forced to find and load the newest version of the program. To avoid this frustration, I recommend using activation group type *NEW until the program is error-free.

The Activation Group *New

Activation group *New can be specified on the CRTPGM, CRTSRVPGM, or CRTBNDRPG commands. Alternatively, you can specify ACTGRP(*New) on the RPG H control specification. When you choose this option, a new activation group is created *each time* the program is called. (The system names it.) It is not persistent in any way.

This activation group is a good choice during program testing. It might also be a good choice for the first program in a sequence, when a long string of ILE programs will be called in batch. The first program can specify *New as the activation group, and all others in the calling stack can use activation group *Caller. Use *New sparingly, however, since the creation and destruction of a new activation group is time-consuming. I am told it is 100 times slower than a dynamic call.

The Activation Group *Caller

As with the other types of activation groups, *Caller is specified on the CRTPGM, CRTSRVPGM, or CRTBNDRPG commands. You can also specify ACTGRP(*Caller) on the RPG H control specification. The program will run in the same activation group as the caller of the program. This is a simple way to handle programs that run "together." There is no need to remember an activation group name. As mentioned above, be careful that the caller is not running in the default activation group.

Before moving on, I want to mention that service programs used by an ILE program can run in a different activation group than the program that references it. Also, during activation, all procedures in a service program are brought into memory, even those not being used by the program.

Scoping Resources

There is a new parameter on the OVR*xxx* commands: OVRSCOPE. It also appears on the OPNDBF and OPNQRYF commands. There are three kinds of scoping:

1. *Call level, *CALLLVL*—This is the traditional type of scoping, used in non-ILE programming. The override specified is valid from the point when it is encountered and for all programs called "down" the stack. If the call level returns to a level previous to the override command, the override is no longer effective.

2. *Activation group level, *ACTGRPDFN*—The scope of the override is determined by the activation group of the program that calls the OVR*xxx* command. When the activation group is the default activation group, the scope is call level. When the activation group is not the default activation group, the scope is the activation group of the calling program. If the override is scoped to the activation group, the override is effective for all programs running in that activation group, regardless of the calling stack.

3. *Job level, *JOBLVL*—With this new option, the override is effective for all programs running in all activation groups, without regard to a call level.

Performance Considerations

Activation groups are expensive to create, in terms of CPU time. Use the persistence feature of named activation groups to enhance performance. If an activation group is likely to be used again before the job ends, keep it in the job, rather than destroying it and creating it again.

Use the *New activation group carefully. It is great for program development, but it is not a good choice if it is being created (and destroyed automatically) over and over again. It might be a good choice for an ILE batch job where the first program specifies *New and subsequent called programs in the batch use *Caller.

Cleaning up an Activation Group

For environments that use RPG IV and CL, destroying an activation group is done with the command RCLACTGRP (Reclaim Activation Group), or by calling the bindable API CEETREC. The API also removes a named activation group.

There is also a parameter option (*Eligible) for ACTGRP on the RCLACTGRP command that will remove all inactive but existing activations. However, it will not remove the default activation group. Also, if an unhandled exception occurs, the activation group where the exception occurs is destroyed.

Displaying Activation Groups for a Job

Use command DSPJOB, option 18, to display all activation groups for a job. For activation groups specified as *New, the activation group name will be displayed as a number.

Summary

The ILE provides the facilities to modularize your programs and get outstanding performance using static binding. You can use service programs and binding directories to "package" your subprocedures and provide convenience for program changes. The use of the proper type of activation groups and override scoping can enhance program flexibility and performance even further.

6

Coding RPG IV
the Modular and Functional Way

Write first in an easy-to-understand pseudo-language; then translate into whatever language you have to use.

—Brian Kernighan and P. J. Plauger

Chapters 1 through 4 of this book provided details on functions: built-in functions, do-it-yourself functions (subprocedures), and C functions. Chapter 5 provided details on connecting your modular components using prototyping and binding techniques. This chapter steps back and examines the programming requirements from a broader perspective.

Analyze the Program Needs

Needs analysis is usually part of high-level program design. It seems that programmers today, however, seldom do much designing. Budgets are tight, work requirements are plentiful, and there is just not enough time for program design.

So, you might have little or no time for a formal program design stage, including the "pseudo-language" that Mr. Kernighan and Mr. Plauger recommend. What rules of thumb can you follow to get the job done quickly, accurately, and efficiently? Here are several:

1. Break it down. With ILE, you can have both modularity *and* good performance.

   By breaking the program into small pieces, you might find that you can use procedures that you or others have already completed, saving time. If you create new routines that could possibly become generic, save them in modules or subprocedures. This will save some programming time in future assignments. Also, small programming pieces are easier to code, debug, and maintain.

2. Use modern techniques.

   Many possible techniques could be included here. Here are a few:
   - Write free-format RPG IV.
   - Use embedded SQL whenever possible, eliminating the use of logical files and open query files.
   - Use subprocedures and function calls abundantly.

3. Follow programming standards.

   Does your business enterprise have programming standards? Are they written down? Does anyone follow them? There is great productivity value if everyone in a programming shop follows standards. I have provided a sample of free-format RPG IV programming standards in Appendix A. You might not agree with me on some of these standards, and that's fine. Make up your own. Productivity overall is improved when everyone follows the rules of a standards document.

4. Get other people or outside resources to help you.

   There might be times when a programming requirement requires skills you don't have. You can definitely learn new information to solve this problem. I have found, for the sake of expedience, that inquiring around the shop yields answers quickly. Personal experience is limited, but occasionally tapping into the experience of others provides great rewards. Questions might include, "Do you know how to determine a modulus-10 check number?" or "Do you know how to sort a subfile by one of its fields?" Sharing knowledge with others is a very good way to improve overall productivity. A side benefit is the inner satisfaction you get from helping others.

Sometimes outside consultants are needed, for complex issues. Learn as much as possible from these contract consultants.

Gather and/or Code the Needed Subprocedures or Modules

Look for routines that are already available for your program. They can be in the form of bindable modules, subprocedures, or possibly just source that you can copy (using /copy) into your code.

There are many web sites with example programming techniques and tips that might fit your situation. Use an internet search engine to find them. While a softcopy of source code might not always be available, you might be able to copy and paste to move code from examples into your program.

Borrowing code from others' work is fair game, up to a point. Be careful of possible copyright infringements, however. In one project I worked on, another firm had a working communications element that I needed. By using a "license agreement," I was able to use their routines in my application.

Even after gathering all the program components you can find, there will probably be some code that you need to write from scratch. Use the ideas described earlier in this chapter and attempt to make modules and subprocedures reusable. Candidates for possible reusability include date management routines, character-string management routines, error management routines, and possibly data handling techniques, such as using "user spaces" or "data queues." Code with an eye toward continued program modifications and routine maintenance. Follow standards for program documentation, including as much commenting as time permits. Just because a section of program is clear to you doesn't mean it would be clear to another person. How many times have you puzzled over a section of an old program, only to realize that you wrote it yourself, a few years back? Write comments.

Although not widely used, consider having peer reviews of new code. In doing this, everyone involved must agree to make the review a positive experience, with constructive criticism rather than negative remarks. Using peers as reviewers increases the likelihood of good, positive comments and a helping attitude.

Use Nested BIFs to Eliminate Work Fields

BIF nesting is a desirable coding practice. It saves unnecessary coding of work fields and many lines of code. The only question is, "How deep should the nesting go?" Using a %len BIF in a %subst or %replace BIF is simple and commonplace. This is two levels deep. Using %xlate within a %dec BIF (to remove currency or other symbols) is also two levels deep.

What about three levels deep? Personally, I am OK with three levels, with some reservations. Here's an example of nesting three levels deep:

```
LongJul7 = %dec(%char(%date(Date6:*MDY0):*LongJul));
```

Starting from the inside in this line of code, the %date BIF takes Date6 (a character field) and uses the *MDY0 format to determine the organization of the digits. The return value (a date) is now the first value in the %char BIF, along with the *LongJul parameter. Its return value (character data type) is the value for the %dec BIF that converts the characters to decimal.

With V5R3 and after, the line of code above could be shortened to this:

```
LongJul7 = %dec(%date(Date6:*MDY0):*LongJul);
```

This is possible because the %dec BIF was improved at V5R3 to allow a date data type to be its first parameter.

I have concerns at three levels deep when it comes to program debugging. The intermediate work fields generated by the compiler are not available in the debugger. I've had to break apart nested BIFs, inserting my own work fields to see what values are being determined by an inner BIF. It's probably not a good idea to go to more than three nested BIFs, based on the debugging problems this creates.

The following are some examples of nested BIFs taken from previous examples in this book. The first example is a line of code that takes an edited dollar amount field, such as $5,362.13, and converts it to a packed decimal value that is the placed in field Amount_N:

```
Amount_N = %dec(%xlate('$,': '  ': Amount_A): 15:2);
```

The %xlate BIF removes the dollar sign and the comma, converting them to blanks. The %dec BIF then takes the result of the translate (*5 632.13*) and converts it to decimal. The decimal point in the character string is used to set the decimal point in the packed decimal field.

In the following example, the decimal field Amount is converted to an edited character string using the %editc BIF, applying the **J** edit code:

```
Message = 'The total amount is ' +

      %trim(%editc(Amount: 'J' : *cursym));
```

A currency symbol is added to the left side of the character string. The %trim BIF then removes both leading and trailing blanks before the result is concatenated to the 'The total amount is ' character string.

This line of code uses the %trim and %len BIFs to determine the parameters of the %replace BIF:

```
NewText = %replace(%trim(NewSchool): Text: i:

      %len(%trim(OldSchool)));
```

Let's specify some values and see what happens. Suppose the value of Text is 'The winner of the tournament is Riverview High School.' From a previous operation, we have found the value of j to be 33, the first position of the school name. OldSchool is a field of 15 characters (whose current value is 'Riverview   '). NewSchool is also 15 characters, with a current value of 'Nixa   '. The resolution of the parameters inside the %replace becomes this:

```
('Nixa':Text:33:9)
```

Next, the %replace removes nine characters at position 33, and inserts the characters 'Nixa' in its place. The value of NewText then becomes 'The winner of the tournament is Nixa High School'.

Our last example of a nested BIF is a line of code the uses the %subdt BIF to extract the microseconds from the %timestamp BIF of the current date and time (from the system clock), and then uses that value as the parameter for the passed value to the prototyped call to Srand:

```
CallP Srand(%subdt(%timestamp():*MS));
```

This is a way of getting a fairly random starting value for the seed of the Rand pseudo-random number C function.

Summary

This chapter is a summary of best practices to use when coding in a modular and functional way in free-format RPG IV. Much of the information presented here is fundamental, regardless of the programming language used.

Many of us learned RPG from mentors, self-study materials, and the "school of hard knocks." We tend to keep on doing what we know works. My purpose for this chapter, and the whole book for that matter, is to raise your awareness a little bit on good programming style, to help you make good use of work done by others (with BIFs and APIs), and to make you more productive overall. If it has done this for you, then producing this book for you was worthwhile.

Have fun!

Free-format RPG IV Coding Standards and Recommendations

Coding standards help make a program understandable to those in an organization other than the program's author. Standards provide the underpinnings of an overall structure, making program change more efficient. This efficiency contributes directly to better quality in programming.

This appendix of standards and recommendations is divided into three sections:

1. Standards

2. Recommended coding practices

3. Programmer's choice

Standards

This section provides recommended standards. Making something a *standard* implies that everyone must follow it, with rare exceptions.

Comments

Comments help document to others what a program is doing. Use comments to clarify, not clutter, the code. Comments should not be used to repeat the content of the code. Comments are done for the following reasons:

- Provide a brief procedure summary.

- Give a title to a procedure, subroutine, or subprocedure.

- Provide a technical description of a programming technique that is not apparent.

A Prologue

Always include a prologue (a brief summary) at the beginning of a main procedure or subprocedure. This comment should be written as a block group. The prologue should include the following:

- A procedure title.

- The copyright. Place the copyright (if applicable) after the procedure title and before any file specifications.

- A chronology of changes that include the date, programmer's initials, reference number, and purpose of the change. Keep the purpose brief. Additional information can be obtained from referenced documentation.

Blank Lines to Separate Related Source Lines

Use one blank line to separate the H control specifications from the F file specifications. Use one blank line to separate the F file specifications from the D definition specifications.

Judicious use of blank lines within a free-format calculation block can enhance the readability of a small logical section of a procedure.

Comments at the End of a Line

Do not use positions 81–100 for comments. Comments placed at the end of the line, in positions 81–100, tend to get lost or overlooked. They might even become erroneous, if the code is changed for a line and the comment is not changed accordingly. If a programmer is using a 24x80 screen layout, positions 81–100 are not even visible.

Code Changes Marked in Positions 1–5

Use a letter designator and sequence number to mark every line of code that has been modified for a particular change request.

Definition Specifications

The D definition specifications are designed to organize all definitions in one place. There is no capability in free-format calculations to define key lists, parameter lists, or field definitions in calculations, as there was in fixed-format.

Here are some additional rules for definition specifications:

- All definitions are to be done in D definition specifications.

- Do not code fixed-format C calculation specifications for definition type items, such as key lists, parameter lists, or *LIKE define operations.

- Use source copy members for prototype and procedure interface statements.

- Indent data item names within data structures, prototypes, and procedure interfaces.

- Use length notation instead of positional notation within data structures. There are two exceptions to this rule: Use positional notation for the program status data structure or file information data structures.

- As a consequence of using length notation, the OVERLAY keyword needs to be used for subfields that overlap each other.

- For compile-time tables and arrays, use the **CTDATA (table/array name) form when entering table or array data at the end of the source program. This form documents the identity of the compile-time data, connecting the data at the end of the program with the table or array definition in the D definition specifications.

Naming Conventions

One of the most important aspects of programming style deals with names that are given to data items, such as variables, constants, and procedures.

Be sure the name accurately describes the item. The name should be easy to read and obvious. Don't make names too long. Name lengths of 10 to 14 characters are usually sufficient.

When naming a data item, describe the item in terms of its use. When naming a subroutine or subprocedure, use a verb/object syntax to describe the process's function.

Indicators

Although free-format RPG IV allows the use of numbered indicators, it is preferable in this format style not to use any numbered indicators. The concept of the indicator, a Boolean data type, is still needed. The use of named indicators is extremely useful; it improves readability and saves any future reader of the program time in decoding the meaning of indicators.

Use the file indicator data structure for externally described files. The indicator name may contain the indicator number, as long as the rest of the name is meaningful. If a file indicator is used for multiple functions, define the indicator multiple times in the data structure, with different names.

Use the *On and *Off figurative constants to set or test the state of indicators or named indicators.

Structured Programming Techniques

Use structured programming techniques to make programs easier for others to read, either for information purposes or for making changes. Follow-on programmers become more efficient when they can quickly understand how a program works. Structured programming techniques provide this capability.

Structured programming involves the use of Select/When/Other/Endsl when If/Else groups get too deep. Also, in structured programming, the beginning of a calculation procedure should start in position 8. Indent two positions for logic nesting, including If, Do, and Select operations.

Modular Programming Techniques

The use of modularity offers methods to organize a large program or an application, and to facilitate easier program maintenance without compromising performance. Use of ILE concepts will affect how RPG IV programs are written, using the following:

- More subprocedures

- Binding directory keywords in control specifications

- Import and Export keywords in definition statements

Character String Manipulation

Character string manipulation has been greatly improved using various built-in functions, such as %subst, %replace, %char, %xlate, %check, and %checkr. Arrays should no longer be used to manipulate a character string.

Use a named constant to declare a string constant instead of storing it in an array or table. Defining a string as a named constant allows for a direct reference to the string, instead of going through an array and an index. Also, as a constant, the string cannot be altered.

The Operation Extender

The (e) operation extender is available for many operation codes. Using the extender disables the default RPG exception handler. If the extender is used, you must code a short routine, starting with If *%error* to actually handle the possible error. If no handling is required, code a null If group with a comment in the middle, specifying why the error is being ignored.

The %fields Option on the Update Operation

The free-format Update operation allows for a %fields option if only a few fields are being modified. The parameters of the %fields BIF are the fields of the record to be updated. If %fields is not used, the entire record specified is updated. Previously, some programs have used the Except operation with output specifications to perform this function. Use the %fields BIF now, and do not use output specifications to perform this function.

Unsigned Integer Data Types

Studies have shown that unsigned integer data types can improve program performance when they are used for loop control (in a For loop) and array indexes, instead of packed decimal.

Filenames on %eof and %found BIFs

By using filenames on the %eof and %found built-in functions, new lines of code may be added to the program near the read or chain without risking errors.

Miscellaneous

Here are some additional guidelines for improved RPG IV code:

- In specifications that support keywords (F and D), use one keyword per line. This is easier to read and permits the addition or deletion of subsequent keywords in the future.

- Begin all H control specifications keywords in position 8, leaving position 7 blank. Separating the keyword from the required H (in position 6) improves readability.

Recommended Coding Practices

This section lists strong recommendations. While not a standard, a strong recommendation indicates that the programming organization would prefer an item of programming done in a specific way.

The %equal BIF after a Setxx Operation

To check for a record's existence, use %equal after a Set*xx* operation instead of chaining. For example, the %equal BIF can be used after Setll to verify that a key exists in the file that exactly matches the key argument(s).

Date and Time Data Types and Operations

RPG has extensive date and time management functions for date format conversions and date arithmetic. Use them instead of mathematic routines and tables. Use the default *ISO option for date and time constants.

BIF Nesting

The use of built-in functions in free-format RPG IV programs will proliferate. It is possible to use a BIF as a parameter within another BIF—again, and again, and again. However, the deeper the nesting, the more difficult it is to read or debug a program. Also, intermediate work fields represented by a BIF are not addressable in the debugger. Therefore, limit the nesting to three levels.

Monitor/On-error/Endmon for Operations Where (e) Is Unavailable

Use Monitor/On-error/Endmon for operations or routines where the operation extender, (e), is not available. Many operations in free-format, including the standard assignment statement (Eval equivalent), do not have the option for error-handling by use of the (e) error operation extender. By using Monitor in advance of the code needing error-checking, the default RPG exception handler can be disabled and errors handled.

Programmer's Choice

This section lists items that are the decision of the individual programmer.

A Comment on the Same Line as an Operation

In free-format RPG IV calculations, the use of a comment on the same line as an operation is a programmer's choice. Avoid having line comments that parrot the code that they follow, however. As mentioned earlier, block comments should be placed at the beginning of procedures, subroutines, and subprocedures. A comment should always be placed *before* the code it is explaining (or on the same line).

Accumulation Operators

The use of accumulative operators is left to the programmer. For example: $A = A + B;$ can also be coded as $A += B;$. The other accumulative operators are $-=$, $*=$, and $/=$.

Capitalizing the First Letter of an Operation

Since the op-code is now first on a free-format calculation line, it is the programmer's choice to capitalize it or not, for example:

```
Exfmt Recx;

Clear Errormsg;

If not exit;
```

Mixed Case within a Name

Consider using uppercase and lowercase to help clarify named data items. Although the compiler is not case-sensitive, careful use of the mixed case can help make your program more readable.

Special Characters within a Name

Many programmers use the special characters _, @, #, and $. While some programmers might not like or use these characters, many others have found them useful.

Do not use any special characters in DDS when defining data fields in a physical or logical file.

B

Built-in Functions Reference

In this appendix, each BIF is described, with a syntax diagram, an explanation of its purpose, and some examples of its use in programming. The examples assume all code is written in free-format RPG IV.

%abs

This BIF determines an absolute value.

Syntax Diagram

```
%abs(variable numeric or expression)
```

Explanation

This BIF takes a numeric variable, or resolves a numeric expression, and returns a positive numeric value. If the numeric argument is either positive or negative, the return value is positive.

Here's something interesting: the data type of the return value is determined by the argument. If the argument is integer, the data type of the return value is integer. If it is packed decimal, the return value is packed decimal.

Example

```
D Volts          S            5 3    inz(-13.8)

D Amps           S            5 3    inz(1.7)

D Watts          S            5 3

   /free

   Watts = %abs(volts) * Amps;

   //  Watts will be 23.460
```

In this example, the %abs BIF changes the negative 13.8 volts to a positive number before it is multiplied by the Amps field. Watts can never be a negative number, so this BIF can assure that this doesn't happen.

%addr

This BIF determines a return storage address.

Syntax Diagram

```
%addr(variable)
```

Explanation

The %addr BIF determines the storage address of the variable argument and returns the value of the address in a pointer. The variable can be a field, a data structure, a subfield of a data structure, an array, or an array element.

Example

```
D Ptr            S              *     Inz(%addr(*IN))

D Index          S             5U 0

D First          S             N

       // Display file indicator data structure

D Inds           DS                  based(Ptr)

D MsgAmount                          overlay(Inds:41)
```

```
D MsgInvoice                              overlay(Inds:44)
 /free

   First = *Off;

   //  If Amount error

   Index = %addr(MsgAmount) - Ptr + 1;

   Exsr check_first;

   // if Invoice error

   Index = %addr(MsgInvoice) - Ptr + 1;

   Exsr check_first;

   Begsr check_first;

   If not First;

     *In(Index) = *On;

     First = *On;

   Endif;

   Endsr;
```

In this example, the indicator data structure is used to name the numeric indicators of a display file. The pointer Ptr is initialized to the address of the regular indicator area. Since the indicator data structure is based on Ptr, it will ultimately overlay the regular 99-byte indicator area. The body of the calculations finds an amount error, sets the index with pointer arithmetic, and then uses a check-first subroutine to set the correct indicator for the first error. If, by chance, the error message indicator gets moved from one value to another, only the data structure entry needs to change.

%alloc

This BIF allocates dynamic storage.

Syntax Diagram

```
%alloc(bytes to allocate)
```

Explanation

This BIF reserves storage in the default heap for the numeric amount of bytes specified in the parameter. The return value is a pointer to this storage. The item to be stored should use the Based keyword and use the same pointer that is returned from %alloc.

Example

```
D Array           S        10     Dim(10000) Based(Pointer)
D Portion         S         4  0  inz(%size(array))
 /free
  Portion *= 100; // Allocate space for 100 elements
  Pointer = %alloc(Portion);
     // The first 100 elements of array
     //  can now be initialized or loaded
```

%bitand

This BIF is the bitwise AND.

Syntax Diagram

```
%bitand(VAR 1: VAR 2: VAR 3:…)
```

Explanation

This BIF performs bitwise ANDing of the two or more variables specified as arguments. The arguments can be character or numeric, but all variables must be the same data type. The length of the return value is the length of the longest variable. Variables shorter than the longest variable are padded on the left with x'00' if numeric, and on the right with x'FF' if character.

Bit ANDing is usually performed with two parameters: a field being processed, and a bit pattern to set desired bits off. By putting a zero bit in a bit pattern, and then doing an AND, the resulting bit is zero. To leave desired bits on, the bit pattern bits would be set to one.

Example

First, here are the rules for AND, for all possible bit combinations:

VAR 1	0 1 0 1
VAR 2	0 0 1 1
Result	0 0 0 1

To summarize: when ANDing, the only time a result bit can be set to one is when all bits in that bit column are one.

Here is an RPG IV example for ANDing two bytes:

```
 D F1              S            1     Inz (x'C6')
 D F2              S            1     Inz (x'81')
 D ANS             S            1
 /free
       ANS = %Bitand(F1:F2);
       // Breaking out F1 and F2 in bits
       // F1 =  B'1100 0110'
       // F2 =  B'1000 0001'
       // ANS = B'1000 0000'   Applying 'AND'
```

The value of ANS after the %bitand is x'80' (not an EBCDIC character).

%bitnot

This BIF is for bit inversion.

Syntax Diagram

%bitnot(*VAR 1*);

Explanation

This BIF performs a bit reversal for the variable specified as the argument.

Example

Here is the rule for NOT:

```
VAR           01

Result     10

Here is an RPG IV example:

D VAR1         S          2      Inz ('AB')

D ANS          S          2

 /free

  ANS = %bitnot(VAR1);

    //     Breaking out VAR1 in bits

    //     VAR1  =  B'1100 0001 1100 0010'

    //     ANS   =  B'0011 1110 0011 1101'
```

The two-character string *AB* is hexadecimal C1C2. This is in accordance with the EBCDIC code set that the i system uses. Following the rules for NOT, the value of ANS after the %bitnot is x'3E3D'.

%bitor

This BIF is the bitwise OR.

Syntax Diagram

```
%bitor(VAR 1: VAR 2: VAR 3:...)
```

Explanation

This BIF performs bitwise ORing of the two or more variables specified as arguments. The arguments can be character or numeric, but all variables must be the same data type. The length of the return value is the length of the longest variable. Variables shorter than the longest variable are padded on the left with x'00' if numeric, and on the right with x'FF' if character.

Bit ORing is usually performed with two parameters: a field being processed, and a bit pattern to set desired bits on. By putting a one bit in a bit pattern, and then doing an OR, the resulting bit is one. Bits already on in the field being processed will stay on, regardless of the bit pattern.

Example

Here are the rules for OR for all possible bit combinations:

```
VAR1        0 1 0 1

VAR2        0 0 1 1

Result      0 1 1 1
```

To summarize: if at least one bit is on in a bitwise OR column, the resulting bit will be on.

Here is an RPG IV example for ORing two bytes:

```
D F1         S         1         Inz(X'C6')

D F2         S         1         Inz(X'81')

D ANS        S         1

 /free

   ANS = %bitor(F1:F2);
```

```
//Breaking out F1 and F2 in bits
//    F1    = B'1100 0110'
//    F2    = B'1000 0001'
//    ANS   = B'1100 0111' Applying "OR"
```

The value of ANS after %bitor is x'C7' (the character *G*).

%bitxor

This BIF is the bitwise exclusive OR.

Syntax Diagram

```
%bitxor(VAR1: VAR2)
```

Explanation

This BIF performs bitwise exclusive ORing of the two variables specified as arguments. The variables can be character or numeric, but both variables must be the same data type. The length of the return value is the length of the longest variable. Variables shorter than the longest variable are padded on the left with x'00' if numeric, and on the right with x'FF' if character.

Usually, bit-exclusive ORing is done with a field to process and a bit pattern variable. If the bit pattern has a one in a position, the effect of the exclusive OR is to reverse the bit of the process field. If the bit pattern has a zero in a position, the effect is to leave the bit status the same in the result field.

Example

Here are the rules for exclusive OR for all possible bit combinations:

```
VAR1    0 1 0 1
VAR2    0 0 1 1
Result  0 1 1 0
```

To summarize: when using exclusive OR, the resulting bit is one if one or the other bits in the operation is one, but not both.

Here's an RPG IV example for exclusive OR:

```
D F1              S             1       Inz(X'C6')

D F2              S             1       Inz(X'81')

D ANS             S             1

 /free

    ANS = %bitxor(F1:F2);

    //   Breaking out F1 and F2 in bits

    //   F1    = B'1100 0110'

    //   F2    = B'1000 0001'

    //   ANS   = B'0100 0111' Apply X-OR
```

The value of ANS after the bitwise exclusive OR is x'47'.

%char

This BIF converts to character.

Syntax Diagrams

```
%char(numeric field or expression)

%char(date or time or timestamp field (:format))
```

Explanation

This BIF converts a numeric expression, date, time, or timestamp data field to a character field. For numeric expressions, this BIF left justifies the numeric value in the return value, includes decimal point and negative symbol, and zero suppresses all leading zeroes. To preserve leading zeroes, use the %editc BIF (described later in this appendix) with edit code 'X'. For date, time, and timestamp fields, the resulting return value will include edit symbols in the format specified on the field.

If the optional format parameter is specified, the BIF will assume the date or time field is in that format. If no format is specified, and no DATEFMT keyword is specified, the format specified in the H control specification will be used. If no format is specified there, then *ISO format is used.

Example

```
D Numfield        S           7  2             Inz(00531.25)

D Text            S          70

D Charfield       S          10

 /free

  Charfield = %char(Numfield);

    // The value of charfield is '531.25        '

  Text = ('The current date is' +

         %char(%date( ):*USA) +

         ', and current time is ' + %char(%time( )) +

         '.';

  // The value of text is: 'The current date is

  //       07/07/2009, and current time is 13:25:07.'
```

%check

This BIF checks a field from left to right.

Syntax Diagram

```
%check(check-list: search-field {:starting-position})
```

Explanation

The %check BIF checks the search field, one character position at a time, beginning at the starting position on the left (position 1, if not specified) to verify that it does *not* contain a character in the check list. The return value is an unsigned integer whose value is the position in the search field, where a character is found that does *not* exist in the check list. If all of the characters in the search field also appear in the check list, a zero is returned.

Example

In this example, a data field contains a first name, possibly preceded by one or more blanks, followed by one or more blanks, and then a last name. The task is to parse the first and last names into separate fields. Only part of the solution is shown here, which also includes the use of the %scan and %subst BIFs.

```
D Big_Name          S          50     Inz ('John Smith')

D First_Name        S          15

D Last_Name         S          20

D Start             S           3u 0

D First_blk         S           3u 0

 /free

   // find first non-blank character

   Start = %check(' ':Bigname);   // stops at 'J'

   If start < > *zero;

      First_blk = %scan(' ': Big_name: start);

      // stops at first blank after John

      First_Name = %subst(Bigname: start: first_blk - start);


      Start = %check(' ': Bigname: first_blk);

      // start now at the position of 'S' in Smith

      If start < > *Zero;

         Last_Name = %subst(Big_Name: start:

                        %len(Big_name)-start+1);

      Endif;

   Endif;
```

This example does not include error testing and handling, such as dealing with a name field that is too long, contains only one name, contains three or more names, and has a middle initial.

%checkr

This BIF checks a field from right to left.

Syntax Diagram

```
%checkr(check-list: search-field { : starting-value } )
```

Explanation

The %checkr BIF checks the search field, one character position at a time (right to left), to verify that it does *not* contain a character in the check list. The return value is an unsigned integer whose value is the position in the field where the character does not exist in the check list. If every character in the search field exists in the list, the return value is zero. The optional third parameter allows you to start the check at the starting-value position instead of the default position of the last position of the search field.

Example

You would typically use %checkr to find the location of the last non-blank character in a character field.

```
D Name              S      20a         Inz('David Farris')

D Last_NB           S      5u 0

 /free

   Last_NB = %checkr(' ': Name);

     // Last_NB will now be 12
```

%date

This BIF converts a date expression to a date data type.

Syntax Diagram

```
%date(decimal or character date expression {: date-format
code})
```

Explanation

The %date BIF converts a decimal or character date expression into the equivalent date in the date data type. The second parameter specifies the format of the decimal or character expression. For character expressions with separator characters, the separator character is entered after the format code, such as *DMY/*. If the character expression has no separator character, place a zero after the format code, such as *DMY0*. The RPG special values *date and udate can be specified as the date expression. If no date expression is specified, the %date BIF will return the current system date. The values for the date format code are listed in Table B.1.

Table B.1: Date Format Table		
Format Code	**Format**	**Notes**
*ymd	yymmdd	N/A
*dmy	ddmmyy	N/A
*mdy	mmddyy	N/A
*cymd	cyymmdd	The c denotes the use of a single digit to represent a century, for example, 0 = 19xx, 1 = 20xx, and 2 = 21xx.
*cdmy	cddmmyy	
*cmdy	cmmddyy	
*iso	yyyymmdd	This is the date format used by the International Organization for Standardization.
*usa	mmddyyyy	This is the date format commonly used in the United States.
*eur	ddmmyyyy	This is the standard European date format.
*jis	yyyymmdd	This is the Japanese date format. Jis means Japanese Industrial Standard.
*jul	yyddd	Jul means Julian, which is a format that uses a two-digit year and a three-digit day of the year.
*longjul	yyyyddd	Long Julian uses 4-digit year.

Example

Suppose you want to process a transaction only if the transaction date is at least 60 days older than today. The transaction date (*tdate*) in the file is an eight-digit decimal, in the format *mmddyyyy*. Note that the %diff BIF is also used in this example.

```
D Days            S           10u 0
D tdate           S            8  0              inz(10102008)
 /free
   Days = %diff(%date(): %date(tdate: *USA):*days);
   If Days > 60;
      // process transaction here
```

%dec, %dech

These BIFs convert a field or expression to packed decimal.

Syntax Diagram

There are several possible syntax diagrams:

```
%dec( numeric expression {: length: decimal-positions})
```

```
%dec(character field: length: decimal-positions)
```

```
%dec(date data-type field: result format)
```

```
%dec(time data-type field: result format)
```

```
%dec(timestamp data-type field)
```

```
%dech(numeric expression: length: decimal-positions)
```

```
%dech(character field: length: decimal-positions)
```

Explanation

The %dec BIF converts a numeric expression, character field, date, time, or timestamp field to packed decimal, without half-adjust (rounding). The %dech BIF converts numeric or character fields with half-adjust. For numeric conversion, the numeric expression can be other numeric data types, such as integer or zoned decimal. If length and decimal positions are not specified, the length and decimal positions of the numeric expression will be used.

In character conversions, the character field may have a leading or trailing minus (-) or plus (+) sign and a decimal point or decimal comma. Length and decimal position must be specified as literals or named constants. Thousands separator characters and currency symbols are not permitted in the character field, but embedded blanks are OK. When converting a date or time field, you may specify the format of the resulting date or time using the desired format code. (See the %date BIF, page 96, for format codes.)

Examples

The first example, which also uses the %xlate BIF, converts a character field.

```
D Amount_A          S          10A      Inz ('$1,234.54-')

D Amount_N          S          10  2

 /free

    Amount_N = %dec(%xlate('$,': '  ':  Amount_A): 10:2);

 // The %xlate converts the '$' and ',' to blanks.

 // The %dec converts the resulting character field to

 //   -00001234.54
```

The second example converts a date to a decimal.

```
D DateMDY           S          6  0

 /free

     DateMDY = %dec(%date( ): *MDY);

 // The %date BIF returns today's date in a date data

 // type. The %dec BIF converts this into month-day-year

 // and the result is placed in DateMDY.
```

%decpos

This BIF retrieves decimal positions.

Syntax Diagram

```
%decpos (numeric field or expression)
```

Explanation

The %decpos BIF returns an unsigned integer of the number of decimal positions defined for the numeric field parameter, or for the numeric expression. When multiple fields are specified, the return value is the sum, difference, etc., of the decimal positions. The result value cannot be negative.

Example

```
D  fieldA            S           5P  2

D  fieldB            S           7P  2

D  fieldC            S           7P  4

D  dp1               S           3u  0

D  dp2               S           3u  0

 /free

  Dp1 = %decpos(fieldA);

  // Dp1 now contains 2

  Dp2 = %decpos(fieldB * fieldC)

  // Dp2 now contains 6
```

The result of six represents the number of decimal positions required in a result variable when multiplying a variable with two decimal positions by a variable with four decimal positions.

%diff

This BIF is the difference between two date, time, or timestamp fields.

Syntax Diagram

```
%diff(end-date: start-date: duration-unit)
```

Explanation

The end date and start date could be replaced by end time and start time, respectively, or by the end-timestamp and start-timestamp fields. The duration unit can be any of those in Table B.2.

Table B.2: Duration Unit Values	
Duration Unit	**Meaning**
*Days or *D	Days
*Months or *M	Months
*Years or *Y	Years
*Hours or *H	Hours
*Minutes or *MN	Minutes
*Seconds or *S	Seconds
*Mseconds or *MS	Microseconds
(Note: only milliseconds are available now.)	

The duration unit parameter is required, and determines what is returned, as a signed integer. A typical error is to reverse the first two parameters.

Example

This example determines the number of years, months, and days since the sinking of the *Titanic* on April 15, 1912.

```
D DateT             S              D       INZ (D'INZ1912-04-15')

D Years             S             3P 0

D Months            S             2P 0

D Days              S             2P 0

D Workdate          S              D
 /free
   Years = %diff(%date( ): DateT:*y);

   Workdate = DateT + %years(years);

   Months = %diff(%date( ): workdate:*M);

   Workdate  +=  %months(Months);

   Days = %diff(%date( ): workdate: *D);
```

The %date BIF is the way to specify today's date, in date data type. The duration BIF %years is used in this example to add a specified number of years to a date data type. If "today" is August 9, 2009, then for this example, years = 97, months = 3, and days = 25.

%div

This BIF is used for integer division.

Syntax Diagram

```
%div(numerator: denominator)
```

Explanation

This BIF returns an integer quotient. Both the numerator and denominator parameters must be numeric fields with zero decimal positions. There is no half-adjust (rounding) available. (For non-integer division, just use the / operator.)

Example

This example determines approximately how many corn plants yielded ears of corn, assuming an average yield of five ears of corn per plant and a total crop of 12,322 ears.

```
D Total_ears         S         9P 0    Inz(12322)

D Yield              S         3P 0    Inz(5)

D Plants             S         7P 0

 /free

   Plants = %div(Total_ears: Yield);

   // The value for plants becomes 2464
```

Duration BIFs

Seven BIFs serve as a convenience utility for date arithmetic. These BIFs behave differently than the others, in that they do not retrieve or extract a value. Instead, they provide a useful means to add, subtract, etc., values to a date, time, or timestamp.

Syntax Diagrams

There are several possible syntax diagrams:

```
%years(numeric field, expression, literal, or named
constant)
```

```
%months(numeric field, expression, literal, or named
constant)
```

```
%days(numeric field, expression, literal, or named
constant)
```

```
%hours(numeric field, expression, literal, or named
constant)
```

```
%minutes(numeric field, expression, literal, or named
constant)
```

```
%seconds(numeric field, expression, literal, or named
constant)
```

```
%mseconds(numeric field, expression, literal, or named
constant)
```

Explanation

Years, months, or days can be added, subtracted, etc., to dates. Hours, minutes, and seconds can be added, subtracted, etc., to times. Years, months, days, hours, minutes, seconds, and microseconds can be added, subtracted, etc., to timestamps.

Examples

The following code adds 30 years to today's date:

```
D Date30            S               D

  /free

    Date30 = %date( ) + %years(30);
```

The following code finds the time eight hours ago. The %date BIF specifies the current date. The %time BIF specifies the current time.

```
D Time8             S               T

  /free

    Time8 = %time( ) - %hours(8);
```

%editc

This BIF converts a numeric value to a character value using an edit code.

Syntax Diagram

```
%editc(numeric field: 'edit code' {: *astfill or *cursym or
'value'})
```

Explanation

The %editc BIF converts a numeric value to an edited character format. Editing is performed according to the rules of the supplied edit code, plus the third parameter option, if specified. The possible edit codes are listed in Table B.3.

Code	Thousands Separator	Output Zero	Negative Sign
A	Yes	Yes	CR
B	Yes	No	CR
C	No	Yes	CR
D	No	No	CR
J	Yes	Yes	- (Right)
K	Yes	No	- (Right)
L	No	Yes	- (Right)
M	No	No	- (Right)
N	Yes	Yes	- (Left)
O	Yes	No	- (Left)
P	No	Yes	- (Left)
Q	No	No	- (Left)
X	No	Yes	Embedded in the rightmost digit.
Y	No	Yes	Put / between date components.
Z	No	No	No
1	Yes	Yes	No
2	Yes	No	No
3	No	Yes	No
4	No	No	No
5	User-defined.	Use the commands CRTEDTD, DLTEDTD, DSPEDTD, and WRKEDTD to create, delete, display, or work with edit descriptions.	
6			
7			
8			
9			

Table B.3: Edit Codes for the %editc BIF

The optional third parameter is used as follows:

- The *astfill value replaces all leading zeroes with asterisks. This is often done when printing a check amount, to prevent check fraud.

- The *cursym value places a currency symbol to the left of the first non-zero digit. The currency symbol used is specified in the RPG H control specs with the cursym keyword. The default currency symbol is the dollar sign.

- The *'value'* parameter is a one-byte value used as the currency symbol.

Examples

The following example puts an edited amount into a message:

```
D Amount          S          7  2      Inz(9786.35)

D Message         S         50

 /free

  Message = 'The total amount of sales in January is '

           + %trim(%editc(Amount: 'J' : *cursym));
```

Here is the result:

```
 Message = 'The total amount of sales in January is $9,786.35'
```

A common use of %editc is to convert a number to a character, and include leading zeroes. The %char BIF converts leading zeroes to blanks, so %editc is often used.

```
D Amount2         S          9  0      INZ(63105)

D Output9         S          9

 /free

   Output9 = %editc(Amount2:'X');
```

The value of Output9 is 000063105. If Amount2 were negative 63105, then Output9 would be 00006310N. The five and the negative sign would be combined, resulting in the *N*.

The possibilities for combining the negative sign and a number are shown in Table B.4.

Table B.4: Possible Characters with the %editc BIF	
Combine a Negative Sign and the Following Number:	To Get This Character:
0	Hex D0, not a character
1	J
2	K
3	L
4	M
5	N
6	O
7	P
8	Q
9	R

%editflt

This BIF converts a numeric value to a character value using floating-point notation.

Syntax Diagram

```
%editflt(numeric field or expression)
```

Explanation

This BIF converts the numeric field parameter to character, using floating-point notation. Two output formats are possible. If the numeric field is a four-byte floating-point value, the output will be 14 bytes long. If the numeric value is any other numeric format, the output will be 23 bytes long.

Example

```
D FP4           S           4F          Inz(1234.49)

D Amount        S           7P 2        Inz(4321.65)

D MSG1          S           36

D MSG2          S           50

 /free

     MSG1 = 'FP4 in 14 byte form = ' +

            %editflt(FP4);

     MSG2 = 'Amount in 23 byte form = ' +

            %editflt(Amount);
```

The results of the above would be as follows:

```
FP4 in 14 byte form = +1.2344900E+03

Amount in 23 byte form = +4.321650000000000E+003
```

%editw

This BIF converts a numeric value to a character value using an edit word.

Syntax Diagram

```
%editw(numeric variable or expression: 'edit word')
```

Explanation

This BIF converts the first parameter (a non-float numeric variable, literal, or expression) to a character value, applying the edit word specified in the second parameter.

An *edit word* is a character mask or pattern that is used to format numeric fields into a form that is more customary. The general rules for the edit word are as follows:

- The edit word begins and ends with an apostrophe.

- A space (blank) within the edit word will be the location of a digit of the numeric field.

- To get a blank to appear in the output, put an ampersand in the appropriate place.

- To get a literal non-blank character to appear in the output, place the non-blank character at the appropriate place.

- For negative numbers, place a minus sign or CR to the right of the place where the last digit would go. At run time, if the number is negative, the minus or CR will appear in the output. If the number is positive, the output will be blanks where the sign would be.

- Leading zeroes in a number will be replaced with spaces (blanks). To "force" the zeroes to appear, you must place a zero in the edit word. This is called a *stop zero-suppression character*. The zero can be used instead of a space inside the mask, or it can be placed at the far left (outside the digits area) to force all numbers and literals to appear. The "stop" occurs after the zero.

- A currency symbol can be placed to the left of a zero in the mask. In the output, the currency symbol will "float" to the left of the first non-zero number. If not placed before a zero, the currency symbol will be in a fixed location.

- An asterisk-fill option is also available. Specify an asterisk within the edit word. Leading zeroes to the left of the asterisk will be replaced with asterisks. This is normally done for check-writing.

- Place decimal and thousands characters where applicable.

Example

```
D NumberPos     S            7  2      inz(9752.33)

D NumberNeg     S            7  2      inz(8631.48-)

D Soc_Sec#      S           10  0      inz(099001234)

D US_Phone#     S           10  0      inz(3095554321)

D CheckAMT      S            7  2      inz(795.51)

D Output        S          120

 /free

   Output = 'The positive number is ' +
            %editw(NumberPos:'   ,  0. ');
   // Output becomes 'The positive number is 9,752.33'

   Output = 'The negative number is ' +
            %editw(NumberNeg: '   ,  0.  -');
   // Output becomes 'The negative number is 8,631.48-'

   Output = 'Social Security number is ' +
            %editw(Soc_Sec#: '0   -  -   ');
   // Output becomes 'Social Security number is 099-00-
   // 1234'

   Output = 'US Phone Number is ' +
            %editw(US_Phone#: '0(   )&   -   ');
   // Output becomes 'US Phone number is (309) 555-
   // 4321'

   Output = 'Check Amount is ' +
            %editw (CheckAmt: '   ,  *. ')
   // Output becomes 'Check Amount is ***795.51'
```

%elem

This BIF retrieves the number of elements in an array or data structure.

Syntax Diagram

```
%elem(array or data structure)
```

Explanation

This BIF returns an unsigned integer of the dimension (number of elements) of an array or data structure parameter. This BIF can be used either in the definition specifications or in the calculations (procedure).

Example

```
D PartID          S          10      Dim(72)

D PartDesc        S          20      Dim(%elem(PartID))

D I               S           5u 0

  /free

  For i = 1 to %elem(PartID);

   If PartID(i) = 'Bracket 19';

     - - -

   Endif;

  Endfor;
```

By using %elem as the value for Dim in the definition of PartDesc, changing the value of PartID's dimension will automatically change the dimension of the PartDesc array. Also, no changes are needed in the calculations when the dimension value is changed. Future problems in maintenance are avoided using this technique.

%eof

This BIF returns the end-of-file (or beginning-of-file) status.

Syntax Diagram

```
%eof{(filename)}
```

Explanation

This BIF returns a value of indicator data type for the result of the last Read, ReadP, ReadE, or ReadPE. If a record is read, the value returned is zero (*off). If end-of-file, beginning-of-file, or end-of-equal group (for ReadE or ReadPE) is reached, a value of one (*on) is returned.

The %eof BIF can be used to check for a subfile end when using ReadC. Also, %eof can be used when writing to a subfile to determine that the subfile is full.

The file parameter is optional (although preferred). If not specified, the %eof BIF checks the most recent file operation.

The %eof and %found BIFs are often misunderstood. Use %eof for checking end-of-file, or end-of-group after a ReadE operation. Use %found after a Chain or Set*xx* operation.

Example

This example shows the use of %eof when reading a file until all records are read.

```
Dou  %eof(myfile);

  Read Myfile;

  If %eof(myfile);

    Leave;

  Endif;

    // Process record here

Enddo;
```

%equal

This BIF returns the equal status.

Syntax Diagram

```
%equal{(filename)}
```

Explanation

This BIF returns a value of indicator data type for the result of the last Setll operation. Alternatively, it can be used after a fixed-format Lookup operation. It cannot be used after a %tlookup or %lookup BIF.

The return value is one (*on) if the parameter on the Setll matches a key on the specified file. The file parameter is optional; if not specified, the %equal will apply to the last Setll operation run.

The Setll operation sets two conditions. The %found BIF can be used to determine that there is a record in the file equal to or greater than the parameter specified. The %equal BIF just checks for an equal condition.

Example

```
Setll  (customer_no: inv_no)  ARFile;

 If %equal(ARFile);

     // Process condition: a record exists that exactly

     // matches customer_no and inv-no.

   Endif;
```

%error

This BIF retrieves the error condition status.

Syntax Diagram

```
%error
```

Explanation

The %error BIF is used together with the operation code extender (e). The return value of this BIF is indicator data type. If an operation code uses (e), and an exception occurs, the %error BIF returns a one (*on). If no error occurs, a zero (*off) is returned. This combination replaces the use of the "low" column indicator for error-handling. In free-format, there are no resulting indicators. If %error is set to one, the value of BIF %status can be checked to determine what error occurred.

Example

```
D Msg            S              50
 /free
   Setgt(e)   (argument1:argument2) FileA;
   If  %error;
     Msg = 'Error when setting the file pointer';
   Endif;
```

%fields

This BIF specifies fields to update.

Syntax Diagram

```
%fields(field1{:field2{:field3...}}
```

Explanation

The %fields BIF is used with the update operation (in free-format only) to specify which fields of the record to update. If %fields is omitted from the update, all fields are updated with their current value.

The %fields BIF can have from one to any number of parameters. Each field specified must be the name of a field in the record specified on the update.

Example

```
Update MyRec %fields(Name:City);
```

Only the fields specified in the BIF, Name and City, are updated. No other fields in the record are updated.

%float

This BIF converts a numeric value to floating-point.

Syntax Diagram

```
%float(numeric field or expression)
```

Explanation

The %float BIF converts a numeric variable (or expression) to a floating-point data type. This might be necessary to provide API or C programs the parameters needed, in the correct data type.

Example

The math function sine, available through the C runtime library, requires a float parameter and returns a float value.

```
H    Bnddir('QC2LE')

D sin             PR       4F            extproc('sin')

D                          4F            value

D Parmf          S         4F

D Parmd          S         7P 6          inz(1.047197)

D AnswerR        S         4F

D AnswerD        S         4P 1

  /free

    Parmf = %float(Parmd); // Convert parmd to float

    AnswerR  = sin(Parmf); // Get sine

    AnswerD  = AnswerR *  180  /  3.14159;  // Get

                                // answer in degrees (49.6)
```

%found

This BIF retrieves the record-found or string-found status.

Syntax Diagram

```
%found {(filename)}
```

Explanation

The %found BIF is used after the file I/O operations Setll, Setgt, Chain, and Delete to retrieve the status of the file operation. This BIF returns indicator data type with a value of one (*on) if a record is found in the named file. The filename parameter is optional; if not specified, the BIF returns the status of the most recent file operation. The %found BIF can also be used after the fixed-format Check, Checkr, Scan, and Lookup operations.

Example

```
Chain (customer-no: inv_no) Arfile;

If  %found(Arfile);

    // Process record...

Else;

  MSG = 'Record not found with supplied key';

Endif;
```

%graphic

This BIF converts a character value to double-byte graphic.

Syntax Diagram

```
%graphic(character field or expression: {:ccsid})
```

Explanation

This BIF is used to convert a character field or expression to graphic format. "Graphic," in this context, means a double-byte character set. The optional second parameter is the CCSID (Coded Character Set Identifier) for the return value.

Example

```
D Company_ID      S            11        Inz ('ABC Company')

D Company_Gr      S            30G

  /free

   Company_Gr = %graphic(Company_ID);
```

%handler

This BIF handles an XML parse request.

Syntax Diagram

```
%handler(subprocedure prototype: procedure parameter)
```

Explanation

The %handler BIF is an integral part of the op-codes XML-INTO and XML-SAX, specifying a subprocedure that will be called by the XML parser. This BIF is required if XML-SAX is used. It is optional if XML-INTO is used. The first parameter (the subprocedure prototype name) specifies the subprocedure to be called during each XML parser event (XML-SAX) or after each set of XML is parsed (XML-INTO). The second parameter is a variable, data structure, or array that must match the first parameter of the subprocedure. The parameter is passed to the subprocedure (by reference) when it is called.

Example

```
D datast          DS
D Name                         20
D  Xhandler       PR        10i  0
D                                           LikeDS(datast)
D  (more parms)
 /free
   Name = 'ABC123';

   Xml-sax  %handler(Xhandler:datast) %xml(xmldoc);

        -    -

P   XHandler       B
D   XHandler       PI        10i  0
D   info                                    LikeDS(datast)
D  (more parms)
 /free
    // handling procedure
P                  E
```

%int, %inth

These BIFs extract the signed-integer portion of a numeric or character field or expression.

Syntax Diagrams

```
%int(numeric or character field or expression)
```

```
%inth(numeric or character field or expression)
```

Explanation

The %int BIF converts the whole-number portion of the numeric or character expression and returns this value as a signed integer. Half-adjust (rounding) is not performed with %int, but it *is* performed with the %inth BIF. The following requirements must be met for character expressions:

- A sign (+ or -) may precede or follow the value.

- Neither a currency symbol nor a thousands separator can be in the expression.

- A decimal point or decimal comma may be included in the value.

- Blanks may precede or be embedded in the value. They will be ignored.

- The character form of a floating-point number is not permitted.

Example

```
D Amount1         S            7P  2        inz(-752.73)

D Amount2         S           10A           inz('1 3 5.88')

D Int1            S           10I 0

D Int2            S           10I 0
 /free

   Int1 = %int(Amount1);

   // Int1 becomes -752

   Int1 = %inth(Amount1);
```

```
// Int1 now becomes -753

Int2 = %int(Amount2);

// Int 2 becomes 135.

Int2 = %inth(Amount2);

// Int2 now becomes 136
```

%kds

This is the key data structure BIF.

Syntax Diagram

%kds(*data-structure-name*{:*number_of_key_fields*})

Explanation

This BIF does not have a return value. Its purpose is to provide a key list for free-format versions of the Chain, Set*xx*, ReadE, etc. op-codes.

By using %kds, the KLIST and KFLD operations are not needed. The named data structure may use either the LikeRec or ExtName keywords, with a *Key second parameter. This data structure is now a qualified data structure, with the subfields the same names as the file being accessed. Prior to doing a Chain, etc., you would load the argument data into the subfields of the data structure. If the file has many key fields, and you want to use a partial key, specify the correct number of subfields in the second parameter of %kds.

Another option is to specify a regular data structure and place the argument fields in the correct order in the data structure. The data structure acts as a key list.

Examples

InvFile is the file the program will be accessing. Three fields comprise the key (high to low): ATCompany, ATCustomer, and ATInvNo. The data structure for the access follows. The compiler listing will show just three subfields.

```
D InvKey          DS                      LikeRec(Invfile:*Key)
/free
    //  Load the data structure from Screen arguments
    InvKey.ATCompany  = ScreenCo;
    InvKey.ATCustomer = ScreenCust;
    // Now Access the file using a partial Key
    Setll %Kds(InvKey:2) Invfile;
    Dou  %eof(Invfile);
       ReadE  %Kds(InvKey:2)  Invfile;
       If not  %eof (Invfile);
          // Process record here
       Endif;
    Enddo;
```

Using the other alternative, you would specify a regular data structure and the calculations as follows.

```
D Key                    DS
D  ScreenCo
D  ScreenCust
 /free
    // Set the file pointer for the partial key from
    // screen data
    Setll   %kds(Key) Invfile;
    Dou  %eof(Invfile);
       ReadE  %Kds(Key) Invfile;
       If not %eof(Invfile);
         // Process record here
       Endif;
    Enddo;
```

%len

This BIF retrieves or sets length.

Syntax Diagrams

```
%len(numeric or character expression)
```

```
%len(varying field)
```

Explanation

In the first form of the syntax, the %len BIF returns the current length (unsigned integer) of the numeric or character expression parameter. In the case of numeric expressions, the defined length or current length is returned. Also, this form of the BIF would be placed on the right side of an assignment statement.

The second syntax format sets the current length of a varying character field. If the new length is shorter than the prior length, the characters beyond the new length are lost. If the new length is longer than the prior length, the additional positions are filled with blanks.

Example

```
D Inv_Amount        S              9 2
D Monthname         S             10        Varying
D                                           Inz('SEPTEMBER')
D Invlen            S              5U 0
 /free
   Invlen = %len(Inv_Amount);
     // The field Invlen is now 9
   %len(Monthname) = 4;
     // The field Month Name is now 'SEPT'
```

%lookupxx

This BIF group performs array lookup.

Syntax Diagrams

This BIF has five different forms.

This form is used for a lookup with an exact match of the search argument to an array element:

```
%lookup(search-argument: array-name {:start-index {:number of
elements}})
```

This form is used for a lookup with a found element being the element whose value is closest to, but greater than, the search-argument:

```
%lookupGT(search-argument: array-name {:start-index {:number of
elements}})
```

This form is used for a lookup with a found element either equal to the search argument or the element closest to, but greater than, the search argument:

```
%lookupGE(search-argument: array-name {:start-index {:number of
elements}})
```

This form is used for a lookup with a found element being the element closest to, but less than, the search-argument:

```
%lookupLT(search-argument: array-name {:start-index {:number of
elements}})
```

This form is used for a lookup with a found element either equal to the search argument or the element closest to, but less than, the search argument:

```
%lookupLE(search-argument: array-name {:start-index {:number of
elements}})
```

Explanation

This BIF group provides a search facility with a previously defined array. The search argument's data type (character or numeric) must be the same as the array element definition. For character data, the search is case-sensitive. Also, the comparison in the BIF group is for the entire argument (plus blank padding, if needed) and the entire element that matches the argument. For numeric data, the algebraic value is used for comparison.

The return value of an array lookup is an unsigned integer whose value represents the index of the element that meets the criteria of the BIF used and the argument supplied. If no element is found, the return value is zero.

For array lookups using %lookup (exact match), the array does not need to be ordered. For all the other array lookups, the array needs to be ordered, either ascending or descending. The order is specified on the array definition. If the array is loaded at run time, the operation SORTA (Sort Array) might be necessary to get the array ready.

There are two optional parameters on this BIF group. The third parameter is the starting index value. If not supplied, the starting index is one. The fourth parameter is the number of elements to search. If not supplied, this parameter defaults to the value of the DIM keyword for the array. Smaller values for the fourth parameter might be desirable, especially if using dynamic storage for the array.

The %subarr BIF cannot be used with a %lookupxx BIF.

Examples

In the following example, assume the compile-time array data is supplied at the end of the program:

```
D State_Abrv      S         2       Dim(50) CTDATA
                                     PERRCD(10)
D State_Name      S        15       Dim(50) CTDATA
D index           S        5u 0
D State-input     S         2  0    inz('MO')
D OutName         S        15
 /free
   Index = %lookup(State_input: State_Abrv);
   If index > *zero;
     OutName = State_Name(index);
   Endif;
```

In the following example, a run-time array is defined using the Based keyword, and dynamic storage is used to store the array data. The data arrives dynamically and not in any order. Since there is a need for a parallel array, the two arrays are defined within a data structure.

```
D AryDS            DS                      Based (PTR)

D Rec                         50           Dim(30000) Ascend

D  Acct_No                     9           Overlay(Rec)

D  Acct_Name                  25           Overlay(Rec:*next)

D  Index           S          10u 0

D  PTR             S           *

D  Count           S          10u 0

D  Argument        S           9

D  Out_Name        S          25

 /free

  PTR = %alloc(1000 * %size(Rec));

    // Allocates space for 1000 elements.

    // Now load arrays via program logic

    //  Assume 800 elements are loaded. (ie. Count = 800)

  SortA %subarr(Acct_no:1:count);

  Index = %lookuplt(argument: Acct_No: 1: Count);

    // Find the element whose value is

    // closest to but less than argument in the

    // Acct-No array

  If index > *zero;

    Out_Name = Acct_Name (Index);

  Endif;
```

%nullind

This BIF retrieves or sets a null indication.

Syntax Diagram

```
%nullind(null-capable field)
```

Explanation

This BIF can only be used with fields that support the null capability and when the compiler option ALWNULL is set to *USRCTL (user control). When used on the left side of an assignment statement, the null status can be set to *off or *on. If this BIF is used for retrieval of the null status, the return value is indicator data type and can be either *off or *on. Extracting or setting the null status does not change the value of a null-capable field.

Example

In the following, assume Date_Paid is null capable:

```
D Date_Paid       S           D
D Payment         S           7 2
D Amount-owed     S           9 2
 /free
   If %nullind(Date_Paid) and payment > Amount-owed;
     %nullind(Date_Paid)=*off;
     Date_Paid = %date();
   Endif;
```

%occur

This BIF retrieves or sets the occurrence number of a data structure.

Syntax Diagram

```
%occur(data-structure name)
```

Explanation

The %occur BIF either retrieves the current occurrence number, or sets the occurrence number of a multi-occurrence data structure. (An *occurrence* is an index.) If the BIF is used on the left side of an assignment statement, the occurrence is set.

The data structure must use the OCCUR keyword for this BIF to be effective. This BIF replaces the OCCUR op-code for free-format coding. Before an occurrence of a data structure can be accessed, the occurrence value must be set. For this reason, I suggest you use the DIM keyword on the data structure, instead of OCCURS. With DIM, you can immediately access data structure information using an index.

Example

This example simulates storage for a two-dimensional array. The first dimension is the data structure occurrence value, and the second dimension is the index of the array.

```
D SimTwoDim         DS                           occurs(50)
D   Array                           9  0         Dim(50)
D   i              S               5u 0
D   j              S               5u 0
D New_value        S               9  0         Inz(417631)
  /free
    //  Initialize all elements to 1.
    For i = 1 to %elem(SimTwoDim);
      %occur(SimTwoDim) = i;
```

```
        For j = 1 to %elem(Array);

          Array(j) = 1;

        Endfor;

     Endfor;

     // To set new_value for i = 31, j = 44

     %occur(SimTwoDim) = i;        // occurrence is 31

     Array(j) = new_value;// array element 44 is modified
```

%open

This BIF checks for file-open.

Syntax Diagram

```
%open(filename)
```

Explanation

The %open BIF checks to see if the named file is currently open. If it is, the return value (indicator data type) is set to one (*on). If the file is not open, the return value is set to zero (*off).

Example

```
FMyfile    IF   E                Disk      USROPN

  /free

    If not %open(myfile);

      Open Myfile;

    Endif;
```

%paddr

This BIF retrieves the procedure address.

Syntax Diagrams

```
%paddr ('procedure-name')
```

```
%paddr (prototype-name)
```

Explanation

The %paddr BIF uses either the quoted procedure name or prototype name to return a procedure pointer. The procedure pointer can then be used for further processing. The pointer is not determined at compile time; it is resolved at bind time. The procedure pointer is defined as a pointer (data type *), with keyword PROCPTR. This BIF can be used with the INZ keyword on definition specifications.

Example

```
D PtrExHdl         S              *       Procptr
D                                         inz(%paddr('ExHdlPgm'))
D psds            SDS
D procname             *proc
D CEEHDLR         PR                      extproc('CEEHDLR')
D                                *       Procptr
D                              10
D                               1       Options(*omit)
D Dummy           S              1
 /free
    // Register an exception handler
    CallP CEEHDLR(PtrExHdl: Procname: Dummy);
```

Enabling an exception-handler program is done with the API CEEHDLR. This API uses a procedure pointer to locate the program to call.

%parms

This BIF retrieves the parameter count.

Syntax Diagram

```
%parms
```

Explanation

The purpose of this BIF is to retrieve the number of parameters passed to the program. The return value is an unsigned integer. If used in a subprocedure, %parms returns the number of parameters passed to the subprocedure. In both cases, if a parameter uses the *omit parameter, it is *included* in the count.

Example

```
If %parms < 4 and %parms < > 0;

   Called_by = 'CA1231';

Else;

   Called_by = 'CA1235';

Endif;
```

%realloc

This BIF reallocates dynamic storage.

Syntax Diagram

```
%realloc(pointer: number-of-bytes)
```

Explanation

The %realloc BIF changes the amount of storage in the heap that was previously allocated with the ALLOC fixed-format operation or the %alloc BIF. The first parameter must be the basing pointer returned by %alloc or a prior %realloc. After this BIF has completed, the pointer may have a different value. This is because the dynamic storage needed this time might not be available at the original location. If the second parameter (number-of-bytes) is larger than the prior allocation, the new storage is not initialized.

Example

```
D Ptr            S            *
D Array          S            10          Dim(10000)
D                                         Based(ptr)
 /free
   // Allocate 1000 bytes for 100 elements
   Ptr = %alloc(1000);
   // Now Reallocate to 2000 bytes for 200 elements
   Ptr = %realloc(Ptr:2000);
```

%rem

This BIF retrieves an integer remainder.

Syntax Diagram

```
%rem(numerator: denominator)
```

Explanation

The %rem BIF returns the remainder that results from dividing the numerator parameter by the denominator parameter. The parameters can be any numeric data type with zero decimal places, but not float. If either parameter is packed, zoned, or binary, the return value is packed numeric. If the parameters are integer, the result is unsigned integer.

Example

```
D Year            S            4 0           Inz(2009)
D Leap            S            n
  /free
    // Leap value '0' means not a leap year,
    // '1' means it is a leap year
    If %rem(Year:400) = 0;
      Leap = *On;
    Elseif %rem(Year:100) = 0;
      Leap = *Off;
    Elseif %rem(Year:4) = 0;
      Leap = *On;
    Else;
      Leap = *Off;
    Endif;
    // Leap will be '0' (*Off) in this case.
    // Had year been 2008, Leap would be *On.
    // The rule for leap year is that if the year is
    // evenly divisible by 4 but not by 100, it is a
    // leap year. If divisible by 100, the year is not a
    // leap year unless it is also divisible by 400.
```

%replace

This BIF inserts and/or removes characters in a string.

Syntax Diagram

```
%replace(from-string: to-string {: starting-location {: length}})
```

Explanation

This BIF has several functional capabilities. One is to remove characters from a string, similar to a keyboard delete, allowing any trailing characters to shift left. A second function is to insert characters. The result is inserted characters, with trailing characters shifted right. The third function is the combination of the two others, both removing and inserting characters. The return value of this BIF is a character string.

Examples

The following shows the use of %replace for removing characters (only):

```
D Text              S           30      Inz('It was a cold +

D                                       and rainy night')

D Answer            S           30

 /free

   Answer = %replace('': Text: 10: 9);
```

The two apostrophes together in parameter 1 tell the BIF there is no insertion. The value of this example is "It was a rainy night."

The following shows the use of %replace for inserting characters (only).

```
D Text1           S           25      inz('Four score years –

D                                     ago.'

D Text2           S           10      inz('and seven ')

D Answer          S           35

 /free

     Answer = %replace(Text2: Text1: 12: 0);
```

The zero as the fourth parameter tells the BIF that no deletion is to be performed. The value of this example is "Four score and seven years ago."

The following shows the use of %replace for both removing and inserting characters:

```
D Text            S      70        inz('The Washington School -
D                                   district won the tournament')
D OldSchool       S      20        inz('Washington')
D NewSchool       S      20        inz('Peoria')
D NewText         S      70
D i               S       5u 0
 /free
   i = %scan(%trim(OldSchool): Text);
   If i > 0;
     NewText = %replace(%trim(NewSchool): Text: i:
                  %len(%trim(OldSchool)));
   Endif;
```

In this example, NewText is now "The Peoria school district won the tournament."

The following shows the use of %replace to emulate the fixed-format MOVEL operation.

```
D Text1           S      10        inz('ABxyz')
D NewPrefix       S       2        inz('RS')
 /free
   Text1 = %replace(NewPrefix: Text1);
```

The operation MOVEL is not available in free-format, but was very popular in prior versions of RPG. In this example, a fixed-format operation, such as the following, is done using the %replace BIF:

```
           MOVEL NewPrefix     Text1
```

The value of Text1 is "RSxyz," exactly the same as the MOVEL. The omission of parameter 3 in %replace sets the default starting location to one. The omission of parameter 4 in %replace sets the default length to the length of parameter 1.

%scan

This BIF scans for a character string.

Syntax Diagram

```
%scan(scan-argument: scan-data {: start-location })
```

Explanation

The %scan BIF attempts to match the scan argument with the scan data. The third parameter is optional; it is the starting location for the search in the scan data. The first two parameters must be defined as character. If the third parameter is not specified, the starting location defaults to position 1.

At run time, the scan is performed by comparing all of parameter 1 to the same number of characters in the scan data, starting at the specified location (parameter 3). If the comparison is "not equal," the BIF moves the search location in the scan data one position to the right. If an equal condition is reached, the BIF returns an unsigned integer of the (leftmost) position in the scan data where a match was found. If the scan completes without a match, the return value is set to zero.

The %scan BIF does not support the array option available on the SCAN op-code. To scan for multiple occurrences of a match, a program loop is needed, and the third parameter of the scan must be used to start additional searches, after the first match.

Example

The following example previously used a %replace BIF.

```
D Text           S            70    inz('The Washington School -
D                                    district won the tournament')
D OldSchool      S            20    inz('Washington')
D NewSchool      S            20    inz('Peoria')
D NewText        S            70
D i              S             5u 0
 /free
```

```
i = %scan(%trim(OldSchool): Text);

If i > 0;

   NewText = %replace(%trim(NewSchool): Text: i:
                      %len(%trim(OldSchool)));

Endif;
```

The %trim removes leading and trailing blanks of parameter OldSchool. The
character string "Washington" becomes the search argument for the scan.
The match is found when the position of the scan is five, and the scan
stops.

%shtdn

This BIF checks for job-end or system shutdown.

Syntax Diagram

```
%shtdn
```

Explanation

This BIF returns an indicator data type of one (*on) if the current job has
been requested to end. If no end request has been made, the return value is
zero (*off).

Example

```
/free

  If %shtdn;

     // Log shutdown request

  Endif;
```

%size

This BIF retrieves the number of bytes used.

Table B.5: The %size BIF for Different Data Types		
Data Type	**Length**	**%Size Value**
Character	1-65,535	Length
Packed Decimal	1-63	Length /2 + 1
Zoned Decimal	1-63	Length
Date	6, 8, or 10	Length
Time	8	8
Timestamp	26	26
Float	4 or 8	Length
Indicator	1	1
Integer	3	1
Integer	5	2
Integer	10	4
Integer	20	8
B-binary	4	2
B-binary	9	4
Pointer	-	16
Variable Len Char	1-65,535	Length + 2
Array	-	Element size
Array: *ALL	-	Element size * dimension
Data Structure	-	Size of one occurrence
Data Structure: *ALL		Size of one occurrence,* number of occurrences, or dimension value

Syntax Diagram

```
%size(variable, data structure, or array {:*all})
```

Explanation

The %size BIF returns the number of bytes used by the variable. For data structures or arrays, it is the length of one occurrence or element. To get the length in bytes of all occurrences or elements, specify *all as the second parameter. This BIF is often confused with %len.

Table B.5 can be used to determine the size of different commonly used data types.

Example

D	Field1	S	50A	
D	Field2	S	23P 2	
D	Field3	S	15S 5	
D	Field4	S	D	DatFmt (*ISO)
D	Field5	S	T	
D	Field6	S	n	
D	Field7	S	5u 0	
D	Field8	S	20i 0	
D	Field9	S	4B 2	
D	Field10	S	9B 4	
D	Field11	S	25A	Varying
D				inz('Altona')
D	Field12	S	*	
D	Array	S	6A	Dim (25)
D	DataSt	DS		Dim (20)
D	SF1		10A	
D	SF2		30A	
D	Size	S	5u 0	

```
/free

// The return value of each of the above

// are as follows:

Size = %size(Field1);              //   Size is 50

Size = %size(Field2);              //   Size is 12

Size = %size(Field3);              //   Size is 15

Size = %size(Field4);              //   Size is 10

Size = %size(Field5);              //   Size is 8

Size = %size(Field6);              //   Size is 1

Size = %size(Field7);              //   Size is 2

Size = %size(Field8);              //   Size is 8

Size = %size(Field9);              //   Size is 2

Size = %size(Field10);             //   Size is 4

Size = %size(Field11);             //   Size is 27

Size = %size(Field12);             //   Size is 16

Size = %size(Array);               //   Size is 6

Size = %size(Array:*ALL);          //   Size is 150

Size = %size(DataSt);              //   Size is 40

Size = %size(DataSt:*ALL);         //   Size is 800
```

%sqrt

This BIF calculates square root.

Syntax Diagram

```
%sqrt(numeric value, expression, or literal)
```

Explanation

The %sqrt BIF returns the numeric square root of the numeric value, expression, or literal of its parameter. The return value is numeric and will be converted to the data type needed for the receiver. No rounding is performed.

Example

The following uses the Pythagorean Theorem of right triangles. (The hypotenuse of a right triangle is the square root of the sum of the squares of the two legs.)

```
D SideA           S           3P 0      inz(6)

D SideB           S           3P 0      inz(8)

D SideC           S           3P 0

 /free

   SideC = %sqrt(SideA **2 + SideB**2); // SideC becomes 10
```

%status

This BIF retrieves the file or program status.

Syntax Diagram

```
%status{(filename)}
```

Explanation

The %status BIF is used to retrieve the file or program status value (a five-digit number) after performing an operation where the (e) op-code extender has been used. Program status values are in the range of 1 to 999. File status values are in the range of 1,000 to 9,999. The value of %status is the same as the status field in the program status data structure or file information data structure.

Example

```
Chain(E) (Dept: Emplno) Prmaster;

If %error;

  If %status = 1218; // Record lock

    Exsr Handlelock;

  Endif;

Endif;
```

%str

This BIF retrieves or sets a null-terminated character string.

Syntax Diagram

```
%str(basing-pointer {:length})
```

Explanation

This BIF either converts a standard character field to a null-terminated character string (used by C language functions), or the opposite, converting a null-terminated string to a standard character field. The second parameter, length, is optional. The length parameter can be used to truncate trailing characters of a string. In the C language, character data type has a length of one. For multiple characters, an array is used, with the last position of the array filled with the null (x'00') character.

Example

The following makes a null-terminated string:

```
D   cString          S          5        inz(x'C1C2C3C400')

D   ptr              S          *        inz(%addr(cString))

D   String1          S          *        inz(%addr(WorkField))

D   WorkField        S          25

D   Char_field       S          5

 /free

    Char_field = %str(ptr);   // Char_field is 'ABCD'

    %str(String1: 25) = 'abcdef';

    // Storage pointed to by string1 (i.e. WorkField) =

    // 'abcdef#' where # is the null.

    // Since the incoming field was shorter than 25,

    // the null is placed after the f

    %str(String1:4) = 'abcdef';

    // Now WorkField = 'abc#' where # is the null.

    // The value in the second parameter (4) includes

    // the null.
```

%subarr

This BIF substrings an array.

Syntax Diagram

```
%subarr(array-name: starting-element-no {:number-or-elements})
```

Explanation

This BIF allows one or more elements of an array to be accessed and used for various array functions. Parameter 2 specifies the starting element number, and parameter 3 specifies how many elements to include in the processing. If parameter 3 is not specified, the number of elements to use is determined to be the elements from the starting element to the total number of elements defined for the array. The %subarr BIF may not be used as the array in the %lookup*xx* BIF. Also, %subarr cannot be used as a parameter passed by reference. To "move" elements from one array to another, the array must match by data type and length.

Examples

The following code sample moves part of an array to another array:

```
D AryTo           S           10         Dim(5)

D AryFrom         S           10         Dim(5) CTDATA

 /free

   // Assume data for AryFrom is as

   // follows:. (1) 'JOHNNY' (2) 'CAROLE'

   // (3) 'EDMUND' (4)'RONALD' (5) 'LINDA'

   Clear AryTo;

   Aryto = %subarr(Aryfrom:3);

   // The values in AryTo are now the

   // following: (1) 'EDMUND' (2) 'RONALD'

   // (3) 'LINDA' (4) (blank) (5) (blank)
```

The following code sample moves part of one array to part of another array:

```
// Assume the example above has run
%subarr(AryTo:4:2) = %subarr(AryFrom: 1:2);
//   Elements 4 and 5 in AryTo are loaded from
//   elements 1 and 2 in AryFrom ('JOHNNY' &
//   'CAROLE')
```

The following code sample emulates MoveA using a based array and the %subarr BIF:

```
D   Ary1            S           1        Dim(50)
D   Ary2            S           50       Dim(100)
D   Arx             S                    Like(Ary1)
D                                        Dim(50)
D                                        Based(Ptr)
D   i               S           5u 0
 /free
    //  The purpose of this example is to emulate a fixed
    //  format MOVEA that moves all elements of Ary1 to a
    //  specific (i) element of Ary2.
    //  In fixed format it would look like this:
    //    Fixed format:          MoveA    Ary1     Ary2(i)
    //  To emulate, first set the basing pointer for Arx:
   ptr = %addr(Ary2(i));
    //  Arx now overlays the desired output location.
    //  Now put Ar1 into Arx.
   Arx = %subarr(Ary1);
    //  The emulation is now complete.
```

%subdt

This BIF retrieves a date or time component.

Syntax diagram

```
%subdt(date, time, or timestamp: duration code)
```

Explanation

The %subdt BIF retrieves a component of a date, time, or timestamp data field. The return value is an unsigned integer. The first parameter must be a date, time, or timestamp data type. The date duration code must be one of the following:

- *Years or *Y

- *Months or *M

- *Days or *D

Regardless of the date format, the year will always return a four-digit number. If the date has a two-digit year in the range 00 through 39, the century is determined to be 20; if the two-digit year is 40 through 99, the century is 19.

For the time data type, the duration codes are as follows:

- *Hours or *H

- *Minutes or *MN

- *Seconds or *S

For the timestamp data type, all of the above duration codes are valid plus the following code:

- *Mseconds or *MS

At the time of writing this book, microseconds return as NNN000, where N is any digit from 0 to 9. Therefore only milliseconds are available now.

Example

The following example uses the microseconds portion of a timestamp retrieval to "seed" a random number generator:

```
H   Bnddir('QC2LE')

D   Srand           pr                      extproc('srand')

D    Number                    10u 0       const

D   Rand            pr        10u 0        extproc('rand')

D   Arrayrand       S         10u 0        Dim(10)

D   I               S          5u 0

 /free

   CallP Srand(%subdt(%timestamp():*MS));

   For i = 1 to 10;

     Arrayrand(i) = rand();

   Endfor;

   //  After this code segment there are ten random numbers

   //  between 0 - 32767 in Arrayrand.
```

%subst

This BIF retrieves or sets a character substring.

Syntax Diagram

```
%subst(character-string: start-location {:length})
```

Explanation

The %subst BIF can be used to retrieve a portion of a character string. Alternatively, it can be used on the left side of an assignment statement to modify a portion of a character string.

Example

```
D CityStateZip    S      50        Inz('Stillwater, OK  73073')

D City            S      25

D State           S      2

D Zip             S      5

D i               S      5u 0

D j               S      5u 0

 /free

   // This example parses out City, State, and Zip from a

   // string

   i = %scan(',':CityStateZip: 1);

   if i > 25;

      City = %subst(CityStateZip: 1:25);

   Else;

      City = %subst(CityStateZip: 1: i-I);

   Endif;

   i += 1;   // At the first blank

   j = %check(' ':CityStateZip:i);   // First non-blank after

                                     // the blank
```

```
State = %subst(City State Zip: j: 2);

j += 2;          // Next blank

i = %check(' ':CityStateZip: j);

Zip = %subst(CityStateZip: i: 5);
```

%time

This BIF converts a numeric or character expression to the time data type.

Syntax Diagrams

```
%time()
```

```
%time({expression{:time-format code}})
```

Explanation

The %time BIF converts a numeric expression or character expression to a time data-type variable.

The possible time-format codes (parameter 2) are listed in Table B.6. Except for the *USA code, the HH in Table B.6 can be a number from 00 through 23. For the *USA code, the HH can be 00 through 12.

Table B.6: Time-format Codes for the %time BIF	
Code	**Time Format**
* HMS	HH:MM:SS
* ISO	HH.MM.SS
* USA	HH:MM AM/PM
* EUR	HH.MM.SS
* JIS	HH:MM:SS

When converting a character expression, the time format code can be specified with a separator character other than the default. This character is placed after the code, such as *HMS/ when the time is *21/15/13*. A zero may be added to the time format code to specify that no separator character is being used, such as *HMS0 for *092911*. For numeric expressions, no separator character is permitted.

When no parameters are specified, the current time is returned.

Example

```
D Time1            S          T
D Time2            S          T
D Number           S          6  0           inz(011750)
 /free
   Time1 = %time('212130': *HMS0);   // Time1 becomes
                                     // 21:21:30
   Time1 = %time(Number: *ISO);      // Time1 becomes
                                     // 01:17:50
   Time2 = %time();           // Current time put in Time2
```

%timestamp

This BIF converts a numeric or character expression to the timestamp data type.

Syntax Diagram

```
%timestamp({numeric or character expression {:*ISO or *ISO0}});
```

Explanation

The %timestamp BIF converts a numeric expression or character expression to a timestamp data type. If no parameters are specified, the current system timestamp is returned. The *ISO code indicates the YYYY-MM-DD-HH.MM.SS.MMMMMM format. The *ISO0 code means YYYYMMDDHHMMSSMMMMMM format.

Example

```
D Number          S    26  0   INZ(192512261303314000000)

D Char_field      S    35      INZ('2009-09-16-1-2-30.00.00000')

D TS1             S    Z

D TS2             S    Z

 /free

    TS1 = %timestamp(Number:*ISO); // Number converted to
                                   // T.S.

    TS1 = %timestamp(Char_field:*ISO); // Char converted to
                                       // T.S.

    TS2 = %timestamp();                // Current T.S.
```

%tlookup*xx*

This BIF group is used for table lookup.

Syntax Diagrams

There are five different formats for this BIF group.

The following syntax is used to search for an equal match of the search argument and the table element:

```
%tlookup(search-argument: table {:alt-table})
```

The following syntax is used to search the table for the element whose value is closest to but greater than the search argument:

```
%tlookupgt(search-argument: table {:alt-table})
```

The following syntax is used to search for the element in the table whose value is equal to, or closest to but greater than, the search argument:

```
%tlookupge (search-argument: table {:alt-table})
```

The following syntax is used to search for the element in the table that is closest to but less than the search argument:

```
%tlookuplt(search-argument: table (:alt-table})
```

The following syntax is used to search for the element in the table that is equal to, or closest to but less than, the search argument:

```
%tlookuple (search-argument: table(:alt-table})
```

Explanation

The %tlookup*xx* BIF group uses a search argument (parameter 1) to locate an element in a table (parameter 2). If the lookup criteria is met, the return value for the BIF is set to one (*On). Otherwise, the return value is set to zero (*Off).

If the return value is one, the corresponding element in the alternating table (parameter 3) is available, using the table name. Tables do not have numeric element reference numbers as arrays do. Tables are always referenced by their names. Also, a table must always be named with a prefix of *TAB* (which is not case-sensitive). Table lookups are often used for existence checking, such as verifying the accuracy of various codes. Tables have often been used for calculating U.S. federal income tax withholding, using the percentage method.

Example

```
D TABState       S           2            Dim(50) ctdata
D                                         Perrec(10)
D TABMon         S           2 0          DIM(12) ctdata
D TABMDesc       S          10            DIM(12) Alt(TABMon)
D OutputMD       S          10
 /free
   If not %lookup(ScrState: TABState);
     // Error - Screen state not valid
   Endif;
   If %lookup(ScrMonth: TABMon: TABMDesc);
     OutputMD = TABMDesc;
   Else;
     OutputMD = 'Invalid Month';
   Endif;
**CTDATA  TABState
   (50 state abbreviations here, 10 per line)
**CTDATA  TABmon
01January
02February
03March
04April
05May
06June
07July
08August
09September
10October
11November
12December
```

%trimx

This BIF group removes leading or trailing characters, or both.

Syntax Diagram

There are three different formats for this BIF group.

The following syntax removes leading characters:

```
%triml(character expression {:'trim-chars'})
```

The following syntax removes trailing characters:

```
%trimr(character expression{:'trim-chars'}) –
```

The following syntax removes both leading and trailing characters:

```
%trim(character expression {:'trim-chars'}) –
```

Explanation

The *%trimx* BIF group performs the function of removing leading characters, trailing characters, or both. Parameter 2 is optional. If it is not specified, the only characters removed are blanks. More than one character can be specified in parameter 2. If blanks are to be removed in addition to other characters, be sure to include a blank in the list of trim characters.

Example

```
D LName          S          30      Inz(' Martin    ')

D FName          S          15      Inz('. .Jim. .')

D Name           S          40

 /free

   Name = %trim(Lname) + ', ' + %trim(FName:'. ');

   // Name is now 'Martin, Jim        '
```

%ucs2

This BIF converts a string to a UCS-2 varying-length string.

Syntax Diagram

```
%ucs2(character-expression {:ccsid})
```

Explanation

The purpose of this BIF is to convert a character string to a UCS-2 varying-length character string. Parameter 1 is the character string to be converted. Parameter 2 is the CCSID (Character Code Set Identifier) to use for the conversion. The %ucs2 BIF may be used in definition specifications or calculations, as shown in the example below.

Example

```
D Ucsfield       S           7C         inz(%ucs2('zyxwtsr'))

D regchar        S           7a         inz('defghij')

 /free

  Ucsfield = %ucs2(regchar);
```

%uns, %unsh

These BIFs convert a character or numeric expression to an unsigned integer.

Syntax Diagram

The following syntax converts without half-adjust:

```
%uns(numeric or character expression)
```

The following syntax converts with half-adjust:

```
%unsh(numeric or character expression)
```

Explanation

The %uns and %unsh BIFs convert the character or numeric expressions in the parameter to unsigned integer (with rounding, for %unsh). Unsigned integers are useful for array indices, loop variables (such as in a For operation), or wherever an integer is desired. For character expressions, embedded blanks are ignored, a plus or minus sign may precede or follow a value (the minus will be ignored), and a decimal point or comma may be used. Thousands separator characters may not be used. A floating-point data type may not be used as the parameter.

Example

```
D Charfield       S              15        inz('+1 2 3.7')

D Numfield        S               7 2      inz(5463.55)

D Ans             S              10u 0

 /free

   Ans = %unsh(Charfield);    //  Ans = 124

   Ans = %uns(Numfield);      //  Ans = 5463
```

%xfoot

This BIF sums the elements of an array.

Syntax Diagram

```
%xfoot(numeric array or expression)
```

Explanation

The %xfoot BIF sums all the elements of the numeric array or expression. If the expression includes an array with more elements than another array in the expression, only the array elements in common will be summed (as shown in the example below). Also, the parameter may be a substringed array (which uses the %subarr BIF).

Example

```
D Ary1            S          2  0        Dim(10)
D Ary2            S          2  0        Dim(20)
D I               S          5u 0
D Sum             S          4  0
D Sum2            S          4  0
 /free
   For i = 1 to 10;
     Ary1(i) = 2;
     Ary2(i) = 2;
   EndFor;
   For i = 11 to 20;
     Ary2(i) = 3;
   Endfor;
   Sum = %xfoot(Ary1 + Ary2);
     // Sum will be all of ary1 (20) plus only elements 1-10
     // of Ary2 (20) = 40.
   Sum2 = %xfoot(%subarr(Ary2): 11: 10));
     // Sum2 = 30
```

%xlate

This BIF translates characters.

Syntax Diagram

```
%xlate (from-pattern: to-pattern: character-variable
{:start-position})
```

Explanation

The %xlate BIF uses the first two parameters (the from-pattern and to-pattern parameters) to modify the characters in the third parameter (the character variable). The return value for the BIF is the modified character variable.

Here's how it works: Each character in the from pattern is compared to the characters in the character variable. If a match occurs, the character in the variable is replaced by the character in the to pattern that corresponds by position to the matching character in the from pattern. A fourth parameter specifies a starting position for the translation. If omitted, the starting location is position 1.

Example

```
D Charfield       S           10          inz ('$1,234.55-')

D Numout          S            7 2

 /free

   Numout = %dec(%xlate('$,':'   ':Charfield): 9:2);

    //  Numout is now 1234.55-

    //  the $ and comma were changed to blank with %xlate
```

%xml

This BIF identifies an XML document.

Syntax Diagram

```
%xml(xml-document)
```

Explanation

The %xml BIF specifies an XML document name, for use with the XML-INTO and XML-SAX op-codes.

Example

```
D Datast           DS
D Name                          20
D Xhandler         PR           10i  0
D                                              LikeDS(datast)
D  (more parms)
 /free
  Name = 'ABC123';

  Xml-sax  %handler(Xhandler:datast) %xml(xmldoc);

        -    -

P XHandler         B
D XHandler         PI           10i  0
D info                                         LikeDS(datast)
D  (more parms)
 /free
   // handling procedure
P                  E
```

Index

** operator (exponentiation), 30

A

%abs, 85–86
  numeric return data type and, 13*t*
absolute values. *See* %abs
accumulation operators, 83
Acos, 24
ACTGRPDFN*, 69
activation groups, 65–70, **65**
  CALLER*, 68
  CEETREC API and, 69
  cleaning up, using RCLACTGRP, 69
  default, 66
  displaying, for a job, 70
  ending of, 66
  named, 67
  NEW*, 67, 68
  Original Program Model (OPM) programs
    and, 66
  performance considerations for, 69
  scoping overrides and, ACTGRPDFN*, 69
  scoping resources with OVRSCOPE and,
    68–69
%addr, 86–87

definition specifications using, 9
pointer return data type and, 16*t*
address, storage. *See* %addr
addresses, procedure, retrieve. See %paddr
%alloc, 4, 88
  pointer return data type and, 16*t*
allocating storage. *See* %alloc
AND, bitwise (%bitand), 88–89
API interfacing, 63–65
  binding and, 64
  CEEHDLR API and, 64–65
  CEEHDLU API and, 64
  dynamic calls to, 63–65
  QCMDEXC, 63
Application Program Interfaces. *See* API
  interfacing
arguments, 4. *See also* parameters
arrays
  elements in, retrieve (%elem), 111
  lookups in (%lookup*xx*), 124–126
  substrings in (%subarr), 144–145
  sum of elements in (%xfoot), 157
Asin, 24
assignment statements, indicator data type and, 11
Atan/Atan2, 24

NOTE: Boldface indicates illustrations and code; t indicates a table.

NOTE: Boldface indicates illustrations and code; t indicates a table.

More RPG Books from MC Press

Free-Format RPG IV

ISBN: 978-158347-055-8
Author: Jim Martin
http://www.mc-store.com/5073.html

The Modern RPG IV Language, 4th Edition

ISBN: 978-158347-064-0
Author: Robert Cozzi, Jr/
http://www.mc-store.com/5080.html

The RPG Programmer's Guide to RPG IV and ILE

ISBN: 1-883884-56-X
Authors: Richard Shaler and Robin Klima
http://www.mc-store.com/588.html

Subfiles in RPG IV

ISBN: 978-158347-003-9
Author: Kevin Vandever
http://www.mc-store/5018.html

The AS/400 Programmer's Handbook

ISBN: 1-883884-48-9
Author: Mark McCall
http://www.mc-store/585.html

e-RPG: Building AS.400 Web Applications with RPG

ISBN: 978-158347-008-4
Author: Brad Stone
http://www.mc-store.com/5015.htm.